I0605592

# HUSH

# HUSH

## HOW TO RADIATE POWER AND CONFIDENCE WITHOUT SAYING A WORD

LINDA CLEMONS

NEW YORK BOSTON

Legacy Lit
Hachette Book Group
1290 Avenue of the Americas
New York, NY 10104
HachetteBookGroup.com
@LegacyLitBooks

First Edition: January 2026

Legacy Lit is an imprint of Grand Central Publishing. The Legacy Lit name and logo are registered trademarks of Hachette Book Group, Inc.

The publisher is not responsible for websites (or their content) that are not owned by the publisher.

The Hachette Speakers Bureau provides a wide range of authors for speaking events. To find out more, go to hachettespeakersbureau.com or email HachetteSpeakers@hbgusa.com.

Legacy Lit books may be purchased in bulk for business, educational, or promotional use. For information, please contact your local bookseller or the Hachette Book Group Special Markets Department at special.markets@hbgusa.com.

Library of Congress Cataloging-in-Publication Data has been applied for.
ISBNs: 978-1-5387-6788-7 (hardcover); 978-1-5387-8188-3 (intl. trade pbk.); 978-1-5387-6790-0 (ebook)

Printed in the United States of America

LSC-C

Printing 1, 2025

*This book is dedicated to the memory of my mother, Louise,*
*and my grandmother Momma Bird.*
*I am forever grateful for how your love shaped my life.*

"Here am I! Send me."—Isaiah 6:8

# CONTENTS

# HUSH

## INTRODUCTION

# The Story You Don't Know You're Telling

Words matter, but your body speaks loud and clear without them. You might think your body isn't saying much as you read this, but as one of the world's foremost nonverbal communication experts, trust me...I can see and hear every single thing your body is saying. In *Hush,* I'll show you how to understand the unspoken dynamics that are happening all around you in any room, allowing you to pick up the silent cues that contain a treasure trove of valuable information. You'll also learn to use nonverbal communication to leave a lasting impression of your powerful persona everywhere you go, and you will communicate with intention and clarity.

It takes only a few minutes for me to pinpoint why you haven't been retaining your best employees. With one look I can know if your husband is having, shall we say…some extracurricular activities. It's obvious to me whether the story he told you about the last-minute work trip is true or if he's running off to sip piña coladas in Jamaica with a girlfriend. In one glimpse I'll know whether or not you like this book while you're reading it. It's clear how you're feeling about your friend's promotion too. You thought you were hiding it, but your jealousy is harder to miss than a neon sign. It's immediately apparent to me if you are genuinely excited about your niece's dance recital or if that smile is a desperate call to be rescued from pleasing your sister-in-law. You didn't finish your work project on time and are making up a ridiculous excuse that doesn't have a hint of truth to it? That will never fly by me. Also, know that if I give you a gift and you don't like it, I will see the disappointment on your face as clear as day. It's impossible to hide anything from me (unless maybe I'm asleep). You've picked up this book out of curiosity, to learn how to harness a secret art that few people have mastered. Or you've had it up to here with your work situation, your dating life, or your interactions with people in general and you are desperate for a new strategy. Don't worry, Ms. Linda is about to school you on a new way to see people and yourself, so that you come out the winner every time in any situation.

To start off my presentations as an international speaker, I pick random volunteers to come up onstage to conduct a simple exercise where, using their body language, I read people and tell them where they are struggling. This demonstration shows how powerful nonverbal communication really is. I want you to imagine that as the hands go up for volunteers, I scan the room to see what each potential body is telling me. My eyes zoom right in on a woman in a red dress who is waving both of her arms in a "pick me pick me" kind of way. She's bopping up and down like she's on a game show and she just won a million dollars. She's bubbly and her smile is as bright as a sunbeam. She's so juiced up that her energy spreads to the people next to her, who are now rooting for her to be chosen. She exudes infectious positivity and she knows how to command a room. I definitely want her up on the stage.

The next hand I see belongs to a tall man sitting over to the side. He's sitting way back in his chair and his legs are spread wide open, encroaching on the space of the people to his left and right. While I'm watching, the person on his left speaks to him. When he answers, his lips draw in, and I see him cover his mouth. No thanks. Those two simple movements are red flags. Mr. Man Spread could be a "Conscious Deceiver," and I don't play with liars. (I'll explain the traits for conscious deceivers later in the book.) But behind him is an attractive young man with a genuine, inviting smile and strong, confident posture. He's dressed casually but stylishly with a brightly colored T-shirt under his blazer, which gives him an appealing, artsy quality. The group he's with is urging him to raise his hand, and after some goading, he finally does. He's my next choice.

Finally, my eyes land on a woman in a pale blue pantsuit. Her left hand is firmly in the air, but it's what her other hand is doing that has me curious. She's touching her "neck dimple," or suprasternal notch, the indent in her throat. It's a self-soothing movement many people make when under stress or feeling anxious and worried. She stands still, her shoulders slightly turned in and hands hovering as if unsure where they belong. Her eyes dart around, searching for an anchor to focus on, and the slightly panicked look on her face suggests she feels exposed or put on display. A nervous flush reddens her neck, and she shifts her weight from one foot to the other as if hoping the ground might swallow her whole. The poor woman is like a deer in the headlights. She'll be my number three, and I hope I can help her.

I invite these three people to join me onstage. After quick introductions I ask them all to simply stand still. People are always surprised by this request. Everyone assumes they must be moving around for me to read their body language, but my style is unique. This book will show you the valuable information that is found in stillness. What we show the world while immobile is often overlooked but plays a huge part in how people perceive us. I observe all three volunteers for a few moments. I strut over to the smiling young man. I move slowly, adding a dash of seduction to my approach. My eyes are open wide, and I have a demure smile on my face. I explain to the audience that I'm certain he is open to a relationship because of his loose, open stance, the quick glances I had caught him throwing toward the other women onstage, and the fact that his hands are a bit fidgety, indicating an excited nervousness—think butterflies. To my single readers, use this information the next time you're trying to decide who to talk to at a party. I inject a bit of fun flirtatiousness into my voice and ask the young man, "So, tell me. Are you single?"

He replies with an enthusiastic, "Yes, and I'm looking too"; the entire room whoops and laughs…he is definitely cute. I laugh and say, "I see plenty of lovely women in the audience." His transformation is instant. Our confident single man is now standing with his shoulders all hunched up. He looks like a turtle trying to get back into his shell and, let me tell you, *it's not an attractive position*. His lips are pressed together forming a line, a silent way of saying, "I'm not happy right now." He's also playing with his watch, twisting it around while looking toward the floor, another sign of discomfort and a desire to disengage. Everything about this man's current NVC (nonverbal communication) tells me he is a mess at dating. To get to the bottom of his issue, I need to tap into his vulnerability just a bit.

I adjust my own NVC. I keep my body relaxed and open, which means no crossed arms. I maintain a soft posture, and I make sure my torso is slightly angled toward my artist. I modulate my voice, adopting a soothing, easy tone to create a sense of safety, presence, and nonjudgment. I want this to come off as an invitation, not a demand. This is a perfect time to use mirroring (you'll learn all about it later) to let my face mirror his concern—I press my lips together just like he's doing to show understanding. I do this because, above all, I want my body to say to him, "You're safe. I'm not going anywhere. Take your time." Vulnerability happens when someone feels seen, not analyzed.

"So, tell me. What happens when you go on a date?" He just shrugs. "Nothing. I never know what to do on dates and I end up just sitting there stiff as a board waiting for it to be over. I never know the right thing to say to a woman." I was right; this man is what I like to call *frozen*. He can't let his body open up into a position of receiving when he's with a woman. I'd bet you anything he struggles to relax his shoulders and open his posture, and he likely struggles with eye contact. This makes it difficult for a positive, fun interaction to unfold naturally. I spend the next few minutes sharing my best advice for thawing out, which I detail in full in a later chapter.

Now I move on to the women, and each of these ladies' bodies is telling me a completely different story. I start with the woman in red whose body practically shouted, "I am available and interested!" When she heard the man onstage was single, I'm telling you, girlfriend, she blossomed like a morning glory on a fresh and dewy summer day. She gently slid her shoulders back, exposing her heart area, which is a power zone in the body. Then in a flash, she licked her lips, and it was so fast it would have been easy to miss. She delicately angled her torso and feet toward our hottie. Now I'm standing right next to her, so I can see that her pupils are dilated. In humans, that's a clear sign of arousal. She is into him for sure. The audience laughs again as I decode these unspoken signals of attraction. If you're single, feel free to take notes, because if my suspicion was correct, even the woman in red, who might as well have been named "the Queen of Flirtation," needed to change her NVC to get what she wanted.

I looked at her with a soft-edged smile, which is a subtle, layered expression that can put people at ease. It's achieved by letting the corners of the lips upturn gently. No wide or toothy grins should be used here. This smile requires barely parted lips to suggest warmth but not total comfort. The eyes play an important role here, and I let them carry most of the concern to complete the feeling I wanted to convey. I let my eyes narrow slightly, showing a hint of tension in the brow area, keeping a subtle crease between them (but not deeply furrowed). This is my way of silently signaling to her that I can see something is wrong.

Think of the way someone might smile when listening to a friend share something difficult, wanting to be supportive but feeling concerned inside. That's what was needed to get Miss Flirtation to be totally honest. "Let me ask you this: Do you want to be in a serious relationship?" She covered her face with her hands like she needed to shield herself. To my expert eyes, this gesture made her seem girlish compared to the woman who stood here with such confidence only a few moments before. She also stepped backward and giggled, enhancing the picture of girlishness.

Here's what the sum total of these physical signs indicated to me: She might be a top-notch flirt, but she wasn't getting the results she wanted. When she removed her hands from her face, she locked eyes with me in a quiet hold. She held steady eye contact, her brows were relaxed, and her mouth was neutral, signaling focus and composure without tension or aggression. "The Quiet Hold" exudes controlled presence; in this case it told me, "I'm not okay, but I am 100 percent open to getting help from you."

Her eyes were also a little glassy, a possible indication of tears to come. She took a breath and said candidly, "I really put myself out there, and I'm not afraid to show my interest either, but it never seems to amount to anything! I don't believe in holding back. For example, I'm not going to wait for a man to reach his hand across the table to hold mine. If it's what I want to do, I'll just go for it."

We spent a couple more minutes talking about how she expressed her NVC on dates. It turned out that what she considered fun flirtation—reaching for hands, deep extended looks into the eyes, sliding closer to her date in a banquette—was coming off as too much too soon. Even if her date thought she was the most alluring woman he'd ever seen, her nonverbal communication was creating a subtle imbalance that could cause the romance to halt before the first date was over. She was not aware that her body was rushing the pace of intimacy rather than letting it unfold naturally. A man could be into her, but what she was doing with her nonverbals was cornering him before he knew what he was getting into. Her overt nonverbal communication could cause a date to want space emotionally and physically.

I knew I could easily help Miss Flirtation solve her problem. I flashed her a big smile. "As my grandma, who we lovingly called Momma Bird, used to say, 'Ya can't throw everything you got into the pot.'" Miss Flirtation and the rest of the audience laughed. "Now, the next time you're on a date, I need you to focus on barely there flirtation." The twinkle in her eyes came back as I explained the concept to her and the audience, and I'll share the details with you later. Finally, I looked right at Miss Flirtation, scanning her from head to toe with a big smile and warm eyes, gesturing with my hand to indicate how lovely she was...both inside and out. "Baby, you're a confident woman with positive energy and you should keep that on full display to help spark curiosity from your date. It's less about impressing and more about creating a subtle magnetic pull. You want him to feel like your attention is a gift, not a demand." Miss Flirtation gave me a big full-body hug while the audience clapped. I'm telling you my entire soul was singing—I had no doubt this woman was going to see a big change in her relationship status soon.

Our young woman in blue was still hanging back and her body was telling a different, darker tale. As I turned my attention to her, she began to fidget excessively, and I noticed she stepped slightly backward, indicating an increase in her discomfort level. Her eyes were cast down toward the floor. Her arms were now wrapped around her waist, closing off another key power zone, the "Core Power Zone," located at the abdomen and hips. Her body was practically shouting to me that she was nervous, anxious, and perhaps even scared.

I walked slowly over to her, mindful not to intrude on her personal space. I looked into her eyes as a tear rolled down her cheek. "Can I touch you respectfully?" I asked her. She nodded, and I put my hand on her arm. "Listen. I can see you've been through something, and I can see that it's been very hard on you." I kept my voice low and soft. "I'm sorry that this has been your experience, and I want you to know that I see you." More tears were released, but her arms were resting at her sides and she was looking straight at me now. This indicated the tension and fear she was experiencing had decreased. I had gotten past her emotional barriers, and an intense moment of understanding and connection occurred between us, but we both knew it wasn't going to go any further on this stage. After a long round of applause, my brave volunteers went back to their seats, and I went on with the rest of my presentation about the power of nonverbal communication.

The examples I shared above represent a single slice of how understanding what your body is saying impacts your life. Being able to read nonverbal communication is like gaining access to a quiet, unspoken layer of truth that most people miss. It lets you pick up on what another person is already feeling before they say a word or even realize it themselves. You'll notice the flicker of doubt behind a smile, the hesitation in a handshake, the unspoken interest in a glance held a little too long. This skill gives you an edge in every kind of interaction, whether you're navigating relationships, building trust, spotting red flags, or knowing when to speak and when to stay still. Once you understand these nonverbal cues, you'll never see people the same way again...and you'll start moving through the world with a quiet confidence, reading between the lines while others are still waiting for words that might never come. Later on, the woman in blue tracked me down before I left for my next event. She approached somewhat hesitantly. "Can I ask you a question?" she said. I nodded yes. "Are you clairvoyant?" I have spoken at countless events all over the world, and I cannot tell you how many times I've been asked this question. I leaned in and gently put my hand on her right arm; I wanted to send a signal to her that I was warm and friendly and open to talking to her. "No, baby. I'm not clairvoyant."

When you are fluent in nonverbal communication, people might swear up and down that you are psychic when the reality is you're just deeply in tune with everything their body is telling you, even if they haven't said a word. Body language speaks volumes. The girl in blue gave me a quick smile and wrapped her arms around her waist like she was cold, even though it was overly warm in the conference room. She was pretty and exuded a gentle energy, but her closed-off posture and sporadic eye contact told me there was something else going on and it impacted every area of her life. "Listen, I don't know exactly what happened to you, but your body language suggests you have experienced a trauma. Your anxiety and discomfort were palpable from your closed-off positioning."

She nodded and explained that she had been brought up in an abusive household and she still carried the pain and fear around with her. Now she was living on her own and getting help and was on a positive path forward thanks to a great support network. "I'm facing what happened and I'm healing, but I don't want my trauma to be the first thing people see! I have so much more to offer." She didn't want to lead with the part of her that had struggled so much and experienced trauma. Like many of us, it was necessary to reassess what her body was saying so she could lead with the version of herself she wanted the world to see.

It's people like the woman in blue who have driven my passion to write this book to help her and countless others who are experiencing these kinds of issues with nonverbal communication. At times, we've all been like her, showing up exuding all our stress, discomfort, and anxiety when there is so much more to us beyond those negative feelings—and we're desperate to push past them and let our inner star shine! There are many scenarios in everyday life, whether you know it or not, when your nonverbal communication is running the show. Left unchecked, NVC can be the cause of four major hazards that will disrupt your entire life.

1. **No one will know the true you**. Your best self will remain hidden from the world, keeping you from reaching your full potential and conquering your dreams. Instead, your doppelgänger will be running around exuding your least favorite qualities about yourself rather than your true essence. Hiding your best self will eat at your confidence as insidiously as a moth gnaws away at your finest cashmere sweater.

2. **You won't get the results that you want**. NVC can be directly responsible for you not getting the result you want, whether that's the life-changing promotion you've been gunning for or a better table at your favorite restaurant. Aren't you tired of looking at a parade of people walking into the toilet while you eat?

3. **You've got ninety-nine problems.** Conflict is everywhere when your NVC is out of whack. You experience constant conflict and feel distance between yourself and others, and you don't fully understand why. This includes strangers, acquaintances, neighbors, colleagues, significant others, friends, and family. Not being able to forge healthy connections can lead to loneliness and even depression. Please, you are too fabulous to be home alone every night eating a microwaved baked potato for dinner while watching reruns of *Law & Order* with your cat because everyone is tired of the drama that circles you like a tornado.

4. **You'll be forced into the apology zone.** The apology zone is a dreadful place where worry and anxiety reign supreme because your NVC is causing problems that you fret over, ranging in size from missed opportunities at work because you blew another presentation to giving off a negative vibe on a date with someone you actually like. The apology zone sucks up time, energy, and worst of all...if you don't fix your NVC, you'll continue to struggle with communication and interpersonal experiences, and baby, it will drain you dry.

I have helped countless people in my decades-long career harness the magic of nonverbal communication. When you are in control of your NVC, you are ensuring that the internal thoughts and emotions you want to express are reflected in your external actions. If you are on the best date you've had with your partner in months, your joy will be transferred to them on a multisensory level. If you're wildly excited about a project you're pitching at work, your NVC can help show competence and shine a positive light on you. Feeling nervous or anxious is human, but that doesn't mean your lingering fears need to be on display for everyone to see all the time! In essence, understanding how to use nonverbal communication gives you the power to green-light your entire life.

I believe my talent for reading nonverbal cues is my God-given gift. I was always intuitive and curious about body language. As a kid, after my parents sent me to bed, I would watch TV with the sound off, and I never had any trouble following the story (and I never got caught either). My ability to hear what people are thinking launched my sales career at the tender age of twelve when I sold more candy than any other kid for the school fundraiser. After college, these skills quickly made me a top seller in one of the most difficult areas of sales: time-shares. Lord, I crushed every quota and then some. My teammates wanted to know my secret, and I happily shared everything I knew about NVC. When I saw how empowering and life-changing these skills were for my coworkers, who doubled their sales and connected with clients on a deeper level, I knew what I had to do. I trained with world-renowned expert J. J. Newberry, founder of the Institute of Analytical Interviewing. I immediately saw how my sales prowess and nonverbal communication skills made an extra-powerful combination. I might not have been in the CIA, but after reading people for over three decades (and studying with Newberry), I can say this: I am the only nonverbal communications expert who is a woman of color. How's that for street cred?

Upon the completion of my training I got to work in an official capacity, launching my own business to help major corporations, public officials, celebrities, and CEOs enhance their performance by adding effective NVC to their arsenal of skills. Since then, I have given countless speeches and keynotes at conferences all over the planet. My clients include major international corporations such as the Coca-Cola Company, Louis Vuitton, J.P. Morgan Chase, Southwest Airlines, Delta, and Google, among many others. And the method I'm going to teach you is the exact same one I share with these clients who bring me back again and again to set their employees up for massive success. My success doesn't stop in corporate America. I'd say I'm personally responsible for dozens of weddings and for loads of entrepreneurs honing their NVC to help get their companies off the ground.

## THE CLEMONS METHOD: IT'S TIME TO CHANGE YOUR STORY

My approach, "the Clemons Method," is rooted in traditional body language techniques but has a unique twist that gives it extra juice. This isn't like other books that essentially focus on interrogation techniques or on only the science behind what our bodies say. Major transformations take place when we learn to connect with humanity at its highest level, and this starts with understanding how our personal weaknesses are expressed nonverbally.

Part 1 of this book takes a deep dive into the emotional barriers that may be quietly holding you back from expressing your full presence and power. These barriers often live in the body, not just the mind, and they show up in three key patterns: "Frozen Solid," where your expressions and body are locked down and your energy feels unreachable; "Flooding," where unspoken emotions spill out of you physically in unintended ways, undermining your message; and "Flat," where your presence lacks the vitality and nuance that draw people in. Before you can master nonverbal communication, you have to melt what's stuck, seal what's leaking, and bring life back to what's gone flat. That work begins here.

Part 2 reveals the powerful, often hidden secrets behind using nonverbal communication to get what you want—whether it's influence, connection, respect, or clarity. This section is about moving from unconscious habits to intentional presence. You'll learn how to command a room without saying a word, harness the power of physical positioning to shift dynamics in your favor, and sharpen your ability to instantly identify deception through subtle cues most people miss. These are the tools used by the most powerful, persuasive people in the world—and once you understand how they work, you'll never see a conversation the same way again. Overall, the tactics and small adjustments in the Clemons Method will dramatically change how you are perceived by others—often instantly.

Anything your body has been communicating that does not serve you...that you're shy, scared, insecure, or worried? Let's replace it with a more delicious narrative—that you are a shining star who pulses with power, warmth, and charisma. Everyone will want to be in your orbit, honey. Get ready for the goodness that will rain down on you when you show up with confidence and radiate power. With total control over your NVC, you'll be able to get what you want—whether it be a top job, a loving partner, or a magnet for business. Strong NVC will allow you to get it quicker and make you irresistible. Go ahead, change your middle name to "Effortless" if you want to; it will suit you. So baby, let's get to work!

Part I

# THE BARRIERS

## How to Stop Struggling and Start Living

## CHAPTER ONE

# You Can't Help It

We've all encountered moments of "the Undoing." This is that unsettling moment when something you did, or didn't do, has clearly caused a problem, but you're left in the dark about what exactly went wrong. It's a silent unraveling, where confusion, tension, or distance replaces connection, and you're stuck trying to read between the lines, replay your actions, and figure out how things shifted without a clear explanation. We're starting with the undoing because, more often than not, when something goes wrong and you can't quite explain why, the answer lives in your nonverbal communication. It's the glance that felt off, the tone that landed wrong, the body language that sent a message you didn't mean to send. In situations where words fail to explain the breakdown, it's almost always the unspoken that created it. Nonverbal cues are powerful—so powerful, in fact, that they can quietly build trust or quietly destroy it. That's why we begin here and uncover how much you may be saying without ever opening your mouth.

I bet you can relate to some of this. One second, you share an idea at a team meeting, but in the blink of an eye you've somehow started a ground war, and you don't have a clue as to what you're fighting about. These uncomfortable, uncouth moments will drain your energy until your spirit is as dry as a bone. What gives? Baby, I know the undoing hurts. It starts with the unraveling of who you thought you were, followed by the gut punch that being yourself isn't yielding the acceptance or understanding you long for. It's that sinking moment where you ask "Why?"—and "What is wrong with me?" You try to exist as you are, yet the reactions you receive feel like rejections, like a silent disapproval pressing hard against your chest. The unsaid spaces grow heavier, filling you with doubt, making you question every word, every movement. You want to understand what you're projecting, what energy you're giving off, but instead, you spiral. Self-consciousness takes hold, twisting your reflection into something unrecognizable. You don't feel good about yourself, and the weight of it compounds, making it harder and harder to move freely, to breathe fully—to just be. In this state, you might as well be wearing a T-shirt that reads "I am an insecure, confused mess."

Seriously, let's get real about what the undoing can look like. Have you ever wanted to curl up in a ball and cry, hide under a blanket, sell all your earthly belongings, change your name, and flee the country because a simple interaction or something you said resulted in an awkward mess? You analyze every word that came out of your mouth and rehash your movements, but you have no idea where you went wrong. You think, "Did I offend her?" or "Maybe she just doesn't like me?" and wonder if it would be better for humanity if you just didn't leave the house. You think about "the Flawless Ones," those smooth, competent people you know who automatically say or do the right thing in any situation. If only you were born with the same big fat charisma gene! You too would have a sparkling presence; be a pro at making fruitful connections; reach the very highest level of your career; have a supportive, loving (and hot) partner and a reputation for solving problems in a snap; be surrounded by fabulous friends; and ultimately fulfill all your goals and dreams. It's like the flawless ones landed here from an entirely different planet! They glide through life effortlessly, turning heads and creating opportunities wherever they go, their positive energy trailing behind them like a cloud of glitter. Then there's you, struggling, confused, stuck, and wondering if you'll ever get anything right. Tell me, does any of the following sound familiar?

You and your colleague James are at a very serious lunch meeting with Ms. Major Client, who isn't happy with your latest work. Losing her business would be a disaster; you feel panic brewing in your chest and have no idea what to do. Ms. Major Client is angry, and she's spewing out a list of complaints while you sit terrified and frozen in your chair. Your face is blank, and your hands are shaking. You start to think about how long it's been since you've updated your résumé (obviously you're getting fired), when James punctures the tension with his silky-smooth and supremely calming voice. He smiles, takes a pause, looks deeply into Ms. Major Client's angry eyes, and gently tells her that he hears her concerns. She eases up a bit. Wow, she no longer looks like she's about to spit fire. James leans in, reaching his hands toward her, indicating that he cares and is serious about getting back on track. She lets out a long, contented breath, suggesting she's calmed down. James takes that as his cue to confidently propose several clear solutions; he offers a doable timeline, and promises to personally check in with Ms. Major Client on a biweekly basis to make sure all is well. You see her shoulders drop and she actually smiles. When Ms. Major Client suggests that everyone order dessert you nearly fall out of your chair. How did James take control of this situation while you freaked out and froze, imagining yourself unemployed, broke, and living in your car with your dog?

Here you are again—this time in a personal situation. It's your first date with Armando. You are giddy with excitement and feel great in your new dress. Your text chats and video calls have been very promising. He's handsome and comes off as kind, thoughtful, smart, and sweet. You take it as a good sign that he chose a restaurant that gets great reviews, and the ambience has a sexy vibe going on. When Armando walks in, your eyes light up and he flashes you a megawatt smile. You're about to melt. The two of you are seated at a corner table, and after a touch of small talk Armando asks, "I'm curious. When is the last time you were in a serious relationship?" Suddenly everything changes; it's like he dropped a bomb on your dinner plate. The inviting smile you had when Armando showed up has been replaced by a bitter scowl. The soft flirtatiousness of your voice? GONE. You've been possessed by the shrillest-sounding woman on earth. You're forking through your kale salad avoiding eye contact. You can hear yourself talking but you cannot believe what you hear yourself saying! "My last boyfriend totally screwed me over. I shouldn't have been surprised; he was a liar and a cheater right off the bat, just like my dad was. My dad was awful to my mom. Total loser. Can you believe this jerk still owes me for three months' rent? He totally messed up my car too. I seriously thought about hiring someone to kidnap his dog; he LOVES that stupid dog. That would really get his attention." You wish you would shut up, but oh no, you keep going and you don't stop. Even worse, your arms are flailing around now, making you look like a maniac, and you've pushed back your chair, creating distance from your date as if he's the one responsible for your tragic dating life and all your baggage. Armando signals for the check the second you pop the last bite of ravioli into your mouth. He dashes out of the restaurant with a noncommittal "I'll text you." Ha! You've heard that one before. You're at a romantic dinner with a hot guy and you dumped all your emotional baggage on the dark and cozy corner table. What is wrong with you?

Girl, you are on a roll. The next day, you get into your car to run errands. You turn on your favorite podcast and begin to slowly back out of the driveway. You notice your new neighbor and her little boy passing by on the sidewalk, and you stop to let them pass. Your neighbor is speaking but you can't hear her. When your eyes meet hers it's like an instant storm of negativity. Her face is cold…her mouth has morphed into a thin, straight line and her eyes are like laser beams directed toward you. You don't know what's going on exactly, but you're pretty sure it means you don't like each other. Before you can figure out what happened, she marches off, leaving you to wonder how such a simple interaction escalated into a drama.

These are just a few examples of how any kind of emotional barrier can land you in hot water. But curiously enough, barriers frequently form as a means of protection—often without our conscious awareness and especially in moments that feel tough, uncertain, or emotionally charged. When you're uncomfortable, your body may shut down, pull back, or go flat in an attempt to feel safe, but that same instinct can block connection and shut down communication. Whether it's fear of rejection, the pressure to perform, past experiences, or just not knowing what to say, these barriers interfere with your ability to stay present and engaged. Instead of meeting the moment with clarity and confidence, you freeze, pour out your problems, or go emotionally blank as the opportunity for authentic connection slips away.

You're reading this book because you're not a hopeless mess. You're a capable, intelligent, perceptive person who is aware things aren't working, but you haven't quite understood why. Baby, you're not broken; you're just blocked. What's been holding you back isn't a lack of ability or desire; it's the subtle, often invisible patterns in your nonverbal communication that have been working against you without your permission. You're not lost; you're just hindered by habits and defenses that once protected you but now keep you from showing up fully. And once you learn to recognize and shift them, everything starts to change. It's okay that you can relate to these examples! We all can! Everyone has situations where we suffer undoings, but you know that the real you won't shine unless your internal world is expressed in your external actions. This woman had a very bad week because she didn't know what she was telling the world with just her body. Her nonverbal communication was all out of whack. A big disconnect occurs when you aren't aware of the nonverbal cues you're dishing out to those observing you, and the consequences can be serious.

To harness the full power of NVC and get the reactions that you want in all areas of your life, you need to know why you communicate with your body the way you do, and this requires a deep dose of self-reflection. This can be hard to face, but a makeover may be necessary if you've found yourself getting the opposite outcome of what you want in your career, love life, and maybe just those small personal encounters at the deli. The Clemons Method is going to change that, and even the smallest areas of improved bodily communication can work wonders in your life. It's time to thrive by permanently eliminating what I call "the Drip of Disdain." The drip of disdain is nasty. It can be slow, almost imperceptible at first—a slight hesitation before a response, a flicker of impatience in your eyes, the barely there downturn of your mouth. It seeps into the spaces between words, stinking up the air with its silent judgment. It's the way you exhale a little too sharply when you speak, the way your gaze slides past people as if they're an afterthought.

A subtle shift away from them, your arms folding tightly across your chest like you can't stand to be near them a second longer.

Or maybe someone is dripping all over *you*. The tap of fingers against a desk, restless and dismissive because they have to listen to whatever it is you're saying. Or maybe it's the impatient bounce of a foot, the stiffening of shoulders, the way their body angles ever so slightly away. Drop by drop, it collects, pooling in your mind until it stains the way you see yourself. You start second-guessing, hesitating before you act, your natural instincts dulled by the fear of making a misstep…again. Or you shrink, trying to take up less space, your arms drawn in, your posture caving inward, your voice quieter, your presence smaller. And yet, no matter how much you adjust, the drip continues. This is where someone else's drip drops us right into the mess of undoing. Their body language brings out your leakage, and next thing you know the entire encounter and what you wanted to convey falls apart. Not everyone "drips" the same way either. Drips seep out in unique patterns, shaped by experience, perception, and deeply ingrained narratives. Maybe your drip is averted eyes and hesitant speech, or perhaps it's rigid posture, crossed arms, or a smile that, as hard as you might try, never quite reaches your eyes. You have your own unique drip, and we are going to figure out where that leak is coming from so we can shut it down permanently.

You know Auntie Linda doesn't sugarcoat things, so here are some cold hard facts. How you carry yourself can matter much more than what's on your résumé. Sylvia Ann Hewlett, in her book *Executive Presence: The Missing Link Between Merit and Success*, reported that "executive presence," made up largely of nonverbal cues, accounts for 26 percent of what it takes to get promoted, often more than experience or hard skills. *Forbes* reports that people who use warm, composed body language were perceived as more intelligent and persuasive, even when their answers were just average! Your nonverbals don't just impact your job prospects either, baby. Negative nonverbal communication (such as avoiding eye contact, closed off posture, or a consistently tense expression) can quietly but powerfully damage both your social and romantic relationships. A study from *Frontiers in Psychology* showed that individuals who are perceived poorly because of their nonverbal communication are more likely to experience social withdrawal and isolation, as they often struggle to read or respond appropriately to social cues. In romantic relationships, nonverbal behaviors are just as critical, as they help signal affection, trust, and emotional availability. A study called "Nonverbal Communication in Close Relationships" showed that when those cues are negative or inconsistent, they can erode intimacy and satisfaction in your relationship *over time*. In short, the way you carry yourself nonverbally can either deepen your connections or silently push people away.

Those sparkling, irresistible qualities referred to as "charisma," "charm," "effortlessness," or "flawlessness," often thought of as innate traits, are largely about how you move, how you connect, and how you show up. This isn't about pretending to have a dynamic personality. It's about letting your body language reflect your capability and quiet confidence. When your presence says, "I belong here," people believe it. And most importantly, you start to believe it too. Could I be clearer about how much nonverbal communication matters? So let's get on with it and examine what's really going on with you—because the drip has been preventing others from seeing the magnificent person you really are.

Whether you're the wallflower who longs to flourish at networking events, the secretary at meetings who knows that he should be a leader, the nervous date who wants to appear smart and sexy, or you are frustrated and defeated because you do not feel seen, it's time to let the inner you...the real you, come out and shine the light. Those heart-wrenching, soul-crushing scenarios belong in the past, not in *your presence*. I don't want the world to miss out on the best version of you when you walk into rooms or make those first impressions. Here's what we're going to do: We're going to pinpoint the barriers that are messing with your NVC and causing your undoing on a regular basis. Once we identify them, we'll rewrite the story your body tells others before you even say a word.

## CHAPTER TWO

# Warm Up

Do you feel a chill in the room? No, you're not coming down with the flu; it's coming from the lady who just walked in: She's a human icicle. Okay, she's well dressed and attractive, but the look on her face is so serious she looks like an assassin. Maybe I'm exaggerating, but you've met this type of person before. Their face is so cold that it can make someone shiver. At work, their unflinching gaze and stiff posture make you think the air around them feels thinner. You just want to say, "Hey, smile, girl." Or maybe you have been the recipient of this obnoxious comment. Could this be you we're talking about? If you're trying to talk to this chilly person, they can cause an immediate sense of unease without saying a single word because looking at their face is like staring at a stone statue. You're also hit with a desperate urge to get away from this cold-faced being. Think of the character Miranda

Priestly, the highly fashionable but iron-fisted boss played by Meryl Streep in the movie *The Devil Wears Prada*. She might have been winning the fashion game, but her body language was almost mechanical, each step deliberate, each breath measured, her presence an invisible force sending an unspoken warning through the air: "I'm not here to warm you up." You don't have to be a diva or magazine editor at the top of your game to be considered cold-looking. You might not be this machine-like with your body language, but there could be glimpses of your inner Miranda Priestly showing during those work meetings without you even knowing it.

Some of the kindest, sweetest people get trapped in the ice. But it's important to know that when someone's nonverbal communication comes across as chilly, cold, or totally shut down, it's rarely about who they "are"—it's more often about what they've been through. Past experiences—especially those involving rejection, betrayal, criticism, or feeling unsafe—can condition the body to protect itself by withdrawing emotionally and physically. Over time, this self-protection becomes habitual: Eye contact is avoided, facial expressions go flat, posture tightens or closes off, and tone becomes clipped or distant. It's not intentional coldness…it's an icy reflex. It's a quiet, unconscious signal that says, "It's safer not to feel too much or be too seen." But what once served as armor can now send the wrong message, pushing people away even when connection is exactly what's craved. Our demanding modern lives don't help this issue either. Both chronic stress and burnout have become alarmingly prevalent. A 2024 report by the National Alliance on Mental Illness revealed that 52 percent of employees felt burned out in the past year because of their job, and 37 percent reported feeling so overwhelmed it made it hard to do their job. These prolonged stressors can lead to an emotional shutdown that leaves a person feeling numb, detached, or disconnected from their surroundings...*making that icy draft feel sharper.* And as you're about to see, that layer of frost can make you seem about as warm and fuzzy as a white walker from *Game of Thrones*...those terrifying ice monsters who bring the literal winter along with them everywhere they go.

Alex is looking forward to treating herself to a nice dinner at her favorite neighborhood haunt. She had a big meeting today, so she's dressed to impress in a leather dress that looks amazing on her, knee-high boots, and her hair is on point. She slides into the only open bar seat and happily greats Joe, her favorite bartender. She orders an extra dry martini and asks how his wife and baby daughter are doing. She's taking a sip of her perfect cocktail (Joe always gives her extra olives) when she notices the hottie from her spin class in the next seat. It's like a switch has been thrown in Alex's brain, and suddenly her kind energy is as crisp and cold as a night in mid-January. "Oh my god, he's going to talk to me." She sits up straighter, her posture steel-spined, shoulders squared off in a way that's all business.

"Hey! We do the same spin class, right? I'm Jacob. You're crazy fast on that bike!"

Alex's heart is beating a little harder; she has certainly noticed Jacob before. He's really cute, and she's a bit shocked that he's sitting right there. She still hasn't said anything, and her face isn't expressing that she's happy to see him. In fact, in the seriousness of her expression, she looks a bit angry, which is the opposite of how she feels! What happened to that gorgeous genuine smile she gave Joe just a few minutes ago? She keeps her body and face pointed straight ahead and does not reciprocate Jacob's angled positioning. This capable badass of a queen who just closed a massive deal today doesn't know it, but her body is telling Jacob, "Please keep your distance."

Jacob perseveres and continues, "Do you eat here often?"

"Thanks," Alex says with a nod. "Not really." She takes a measured breath, which makes her look like she's about to scold a child; in reality she's thinking about how strong Jacob's calves look as he pushes himself on his bike. She wants to connect and has been single for four years, but she can't relax enough to mirror his inviting positioning and easygoing manner of chatting. He moves in a little closer. She notices that Jacob smells great, but she stays frozen in her seat. He speaks again: "I've never been here. Any dishes you recommend?"

"The chicken is good," Alex says with a matter-of-fact tone. Her voice is low and even, devoid of warmth, as if emotions were extras she has stopped bothering with. She makes eye contact with him for about a second, before returning her gaze forward. Suddenly Jacob hops up and says, "Okay. Actually, I think I'm going to grab a table. Have a good night." In a flash he's gone, leaving Alex to order the same old chicken and eat it by herself. It's like this every time she talks to a man: Nothing happens, and she desperately wants to go out on some dates.

Later that week Alex walks into the gym and there's Jacob, smiling at her. "Hey! Alex! I'm going to check out the kettlebell class. Want to give it a try? It's supposed to be a great workout." Alex's face remains blank as she tries to compute in her head what she should say this time while Cutie waits for a response. It's as if she's frozen…again. She does manage to look at him, but she doesn't manage to smile like she did at the woman at the front desk who checked her in. Finally, she realizes, "I'm doing spin. Sorry." Jacob shrugs, his smile vanishing. "Yeah. Okay, see you around," he says, then walks away without looking at her. Alex can't believe she just blew that: "What did I do? Is he angry with me because I won't go to his class?" Clearly, she could have done something to let him know she was attracted to him! But she's horrible at flirting and has flunked again. After class she walks home, opens the door to her apartment, and is greeted by Cinnabon, her beloved beagle who is happily wagging his tail. Sometimes it feels like he is the only creature on earth who truly understands her.

## BARRIER #1: FROZEN SOLID

> ***Frozen Solid:*** *Individuals who either intentionally or unconsciously restrict their emotional expression, social interactions, and state of openness, which leads to an inability to make meaningful connections with others. They come off as icy cold, and this can result in*

*misunderstandings, missed opportunities, and unnecessary conflict.*

***The tired, old excuse:*** *"No one gets me. I'm just not a people person."*

Alex may think no one gets her, but her problems all stem from the same issue. Alex is the poster child for Barrier #1; the girl is frozen solid. Everything about her is icy, and she needs to defrost her entire body from head to toe if she wants to make authentic human connections. The reality is Alex is an intelligent, attractive young professional who has many wonderful qualities. She volunteers to work with rescue dogs, is rising in the ranks at her company, and crochets beautiful scarves for all her friends. You'd never know it, though, because everything about her is so shut down. Alex isn't unfriendly or uncaring—it's just that her chilly outside presentation does not match her warm interior. At heart she is polite and respectful, but icy cold people are accustomed to keeping interactions completely controlled. Trusting others doesn't come easily either, so they often build emotional walls that are so high only Spider-Man could climb over them. People who are frozen are often stuck in the present and are unable to face any kind of change. Risk-taking or even sticking a single frostbitten toe outside the cold box Alex has confined herself in feels like an undertaking on a par with summiting Mount Everest. Being closed up and distant can lead to loneliness, isolation, frustration, and feeling misunderstood by people in your life (except maybe your dog). Let's take a look at the other traits folks who need to warm up are exhibiting.

Colleen has always wondered why people are so hard on her. The poor girl has no idea that, as she goes about her day, people are simply matching her energy, and her energy is so mighty and forceful it's like something out of Greek mythology. Colleen is like Medusa. Anyone who dared to meet Medusa's gaze was turned *into stone.* Colleen's Medusa complex has an immediate effect on people that causes everyone she encounters to be rude to her. It happens everywhere—coffee shops, restaurants, even the grocery store. Baristas barely look at her, servers seem eager to rush her out, and cashiers never make small talk the way they do with other customers. She notices how they laugh and chat with the people ahead of her in line, but the moment it's her turn, their smiles fade; their voices become flat. It isn't fair. She is polite. She never snaps or raises her voice. She was raised right! She always says "please" and "thank you." So why does the world seem to greet her with indifference? This morning had been no different. Colleen had ordered a latte, only to have the barista hand it to her without so much as a glance. No "Have a nice day," not even a friendly nod! Just a silent transaction, like she wasn't even there. As she took her drink and walked away, she felt the sting of it. Maybe people were just colder these days. Maybe customer service just wasn't what it used to be. But deep down, there was a nagging thought she quickly pushed away—was something wrong with her?

What's *wrong* with poor Colleen is that she stands with her back rigid and her arms stiff at her sides like a statue. Her lips stay pressed into a tight, unreadable line, and her gaze, direct but vacant, makes people feel as if they need to get out of her line of sight immediately. A blank face that is impossible to read can be as off-putting as the nastiest look anyone has ever given you. A blank face is often associated with someone who is standoffish, apathetic, or at its worst, *mean*. Human beings are wired to seek emotional feedback from others—when we get nothing, our brains struggle to interpret the person's intentions, making us feel uneasy or even threatened. A stony face like Colleen's creates a psychological barrier, signaling detachment or disinterest. It can also trigger defensive reactions, as people tend to mirror emotions to build rapport. Without any cues of warmth or openness, interactions can quickly become strained, leaving the other person feeling rejected, judged, or unwelcomed. While Colleen's words to the barista were polite when she ordered her latte, her demeanor sent a different message entirely: "I'm not here to connect. Just do your job." And so people did. They gave her what she seemed to expect—nothing more, nothing less. And Colleen, unaware of her impact on people, left every encounter feeling…cold.

## LET'S FACE IT, ERASE IT, AND REPLACE IT

Being frozen solid is as unpleasant as it sounds—it's a cold, dark, lonely, and miserable place to be. If Alex doesn't break through this barrier, her life will continue to look like a frozen tundra. It will hold her back from experiencing growth personally or professionally. It will be harder to create new relationships. Poor Colleen's body and face are so frozen, and her eyes so blank, that *people literally can't tell if anyone is in there.* She's as cold as a stone, and people aren't interested in being around her. Girlfriend is stuck on her own personal ice floe and has no clue how to navigate to a place where the temperatures rise above freezing. The good news is that when someone is frozen solid, shifting nonverbal communication in a few key areas will allow them to warm up and break through this barrier. Now, I know it's hard to break these strongly ingrained habits—but follow my advice and you'll shed these layers of ice, revealing an entirely new you.

To warm you up, let's first take a look at how you're using your "Heart Power Zone" (one of the three power zones of NVC, along with "the Head" and "the Core," which will be covered later on). The heart power zone refers to your chest area, and the space from the collarbone to the lower rib cage is especially important—yes, baby, it's the place where your heart is located. When people talk about someone "leading with her heart" or "having an open heart," they are often referring to this power zone. The heart power zone represents authenticity, sincerity, and emotional connection, so it plays a crucial role in building trust and rapport. No one maximizes this more than Oprah Winfrey. Her open chest, relaxed shoulders, and expressive hand gestures…often originating from her heart, help her connect deeply with audiences.

Whether she's conducting an emotional interview or giving a motivational speech, she maintains an open posture that exudes warmth and sincerity. Her use of expansive gestures and hand-over-heart movements reinforces trust and makes her audience feel valued and understood. We can all learn a lesson from Oprah. When the heart power zone is activated, it presents a picture of confidence, warmth, and approachability. It's a means of projecting self-assurance without arrogance, making a person appear both powerful *and* emotionally available. It's the posture of someone who is comfortable in their own skin and ready to engage with the world. When your heart power zone is wide open you radiate a magical, magnetic power that people are instantly drawn to.

To activate your heart power, start with the posture first. You want to roll your shoulders back and down, allowing your chest to expand naturally. Be sure to stand tall with a strong yet relaxed spine. This open stance will instantly signal confidence and approachability. The arms are loose and natural, not crossed or clenched, signaling openness to connection. Your hands should be relaxed, occasionally gesturing during conversation to emphasize points, reinforcing engagement and openness. Hand gestures originating from the heart, such as placing a hand over the chest, open palms, or expansive gestures, can reinforce a feeling of sincerity and strengthen connections while putting others at ease. If you're ever unsure about what to do with your hands, an easy technique is to place a hand on your heart. Placing a hand directly on your heart helps reinforce the habit of opening this zone to project sincerity and gratitude. This movement is especially useful when engaged in one-on-one conversation, as it indicates a deep, emotional connection to what is being said. Start making a point to put your hand on your heart and lean in, as this is a quick, almost effortless way to demonstrate your warmth and openness to others.

You need just the right amount of eye contact here too. Direct eye contact is one of the most powerful nonverbal cues we have. Many icy cold people struggle to make direct eye contact during conversations. This announces that they are uncomfortable, anxious, or nervous in someone's presence, and it comes off as unwelcoming. A lack of eye contact can also suggest distraction, disinterest, or even dishonesty, making the listener feel unimportant or dismissed, which makes an authentic connection practically impossible. Those who are truly arctic in their demeanor have what I refer to as stone-cold eyes. Their eyes are vacant, which can be a signal of detachment or internal distress, leaving the other person feeling as though they are speaking into a dark void during a conversation. Melania Trump stares straight ahead in public appearances and her stare feels icily unreadable—it's nearly impossible to tell exactly what she's thinking. In court sketches of Ghislaine Maxwell, who was sentenced to twenty years in prison for her role in facilitating Jeffrey Epstein's abuse of minor girls, her gaze was often cold, blank, or downright eerie. There's an unnerving stillness—no warmth, not a flicker of emotion. Vladimir Putin's impassive stare also has a chilling effect. These forms of stone-cold eyes suggest calculated control (they don't want to reveal emotion), dissociation (they're not fully present), and sometimes even supremacy (a belief they're above the situation or people around them).

When individuals display stone-cold eyes it often evokes feelings of discomfort, unease, and sometimes fear in observers. This reaction stems from the human tendency to seek connection through eye contact, a fundamental aspect of nonverbal communication. When this expected flicker of life is absent, you have a problem. According to a September 2024 article by the NeuroLaunch editorial team, research indicates that people may perceive individuals with vacant gazes as unfriendly, disinterested, *or even dangerous*. No wonder Colleen didn't get a "Have a good day" after buying her latte like the customer before her.

To eliminate stone-cold eyes, first, focus solely on *seeing* the person in front of you. You've got to register their presence with your eyes. Engage by slightly widening your eyes, maintaining steady but warm eye contact, and letting your gaze subtly respond to the flow of the discussion, showing curiosity and presence rather than detachment. Maintain a steady, warm gaze without staring too intensely, signaling confidence and attentiveness. Mind you, it's not a staring contest; it's normal to blink and look away. To help execute this properly, simply think of a few things that bring you joy as you engage in conversation. Picture an adorable golden retriever puppy, a basket of kittens, your child, a perfect ice cream cone, a beautiful flower...*anything* that will uplift you and bring warmth to your eyes. While you're imagining that precious puppy, you also need to keep your facial expression soft and approachable. A subtle smile or a relaxed mouth enhances the impact you're trying to make.

Deep, even breathing helps here too. Allowing your chest to expand will prevent tension from creeping into your shoulders. Shallow breaths can make you appear uneasy (or like you're having a panic attack), whereas controlled breathing exudes calm self-assurance with the added benefit of keeping *you* relaxed. Now, a slight lean-in when listening conveys an extra dose of interest. Leaning too far back should be avoided, as you'll just look distant and bored, like you can't wait to get home and binge some Shonda Rhimes. The slight lean-in also makes the person you are talking to feel special, as if you've aimed your own personal spotlight right on them. This ignites a connection that grows into accessibility and warmth.

Finally, own your space with confidence, and move with intentionality—whether it's a purposeful stride or a deliberate gesture. When you embody your heart power zone fully, you strike the perfect balance between strength and making yourself more magnetic, approachable, and effortlessly commanding in any interaction. Look at any leader, dazzling celebrity, or the strongest communicator at your job, and you'll see they operate with their heart power zone open wide.

Jacinda Ardern, former prime minister of New Zealand, embodies heart power presence with her relaxed posture, open gestures, and direct yet soft eye contact. Her body language consistently reflects calm authority and genuine care, with an open chest and expressive hands that reinforce connection. She leads with empathy and clarity, balancing warmth with strength in a way that earns trust and respect.

Keanu Reeves demonstrates strong heart power zone presence through relaxed shoulders, open chest, and calm, steady eye contact. His body language is centered and grounded, signaling emotional availability and quiet confidence. The confidence is evident, but there's also an air of self-assuredness, trustworthiness, and approachability. That's the heart power in action. It dazzles, soothes, impresses, and baby, it will take you places.

People who are frozen solid tend to resort to "Short Answer Syndrome" when speaking to others. They gravitate toward a limited verbal expression, featuring vague, incredibly basic responses such as "It's fine" or "Okay," and this can end a conversation before it begins.[1] Communicating with such drab, boring phrases makes a conversation feel one-sided and exhausting for the person on the other side. We've all been there…you're trying to make conversation with the person seated next to you at a dinner party. "Hi. I'm Linda. How do you know our hostess?" "Work." The bland reply puts a halt to

1. I know we're focusing on nonverbal communication, but when life requires that we open our mouths and speak, sometimes tone, cadence, or speech patterns make a barrier even harder to get over.

the flow of conversation. You might try again: "Okay, what do you do?" "Sales." Another dead-end response. You take a sip of your cocktail in defeat and move on in hopes of finding a livelier person to talk to.

A side effect of short answer syndrome is that it prevents a person from sharing any personal thoughts or details about themselves. Think of the expression "It was like talking to a wall." Whoever coined this expression clearly knew some icy cold people because walls have zero personality, and they don't talk back either. In Alex's case, Jacob had angled his body toward her to indicate he was open to a chat (and perhaps a date), but her short and uninspired answer, "The chicken is good," came off as curt, so Jacob interpreted her answer as an attempt to get rid of him. Short answer syndrome can severely limit every aspect of your life because it sends out a constant signal that you aren't interested in talking with anyone for any reason. Period. Getting over this syndrome brings real benefits that go beyond improving your dating and job prospects. A 2014 study from the University of Chicago found that talking to strangers and acquaintances improves mood and feelings of connection, often more than people expect. In this study people predicted that they'd *feel awkward* but reported higher happiness after casual conversations. A 2010 study published in *Social Psychological and Personality Science* found that, in addition to an extra jolt of happiness, engaging in brief social interaction before a task improved cognitive performance. Participants who made small talk before a test scored significantly higher than those who didn't! The study likened small talk to warming up the brain just like stretching before a workout. So go get yourself out there!

Low-stakes environments are your practice field. I'd like you to start implementing these skills as habits in your everyday life, starting today...right now if you're reading this in public. You're going to be mindful of opening your heart power zone while chatting up cashiers, other people in line, your technician at the nail salon; and when pumping gas, putting on lipstick next to coworkers you see in the restroom, and so forth. I know your face is squeezing up right now and you're wincing at this idea, but we need to cross Barrier #1, and practice is needed in order to build the muscle. If you make an awkward misstep while talking with the woman in front of you at Starbucks, do you really need to care? No, you do not. Practicing how to talk to people when you feel frozen is like exercising a muscle—the more you do it, the stronger and more natural it becomes. At first it might feel awkward, overwhelming, or even terrifying, but with each small attempt, you're rewiring your nervous system to recognize that you're safe and capable.

Over time, what once felt impossible starts to feel manageable, even empowering. The fear doesn't necessarily vanish overnight, but your confidence grows as you prove to yourself, again and again, that you can show up, speak up, and connect—even when it's hard or you feel afraid. As you become more adept at conversation you can gradually increase the complexity and length of your interactions, making this muscle even stronger. Simply talking to another person, even if only for a few seconds, is a gateway to having more in-depth and personal conversations with anyone. If you're breaking out in hives just thinking about having to spark up conversations with strangers, relax! I have some specific suggestions to get you through it.

Yes-or-no questions and answers are conversation killers, and unless you're being deposed in a court of law, they should be eliminated from your vocabulary. Practice using open-ended questions that encourage the other person to keep the conversation moving forward. And baby, there is nothing wrong with arming yourself in advance with a few topics or questions to help you steer a conversation. Think mutual interests, current events, family, food, popular culture (who doesn't like talking about sports or reality TV?). Eliminating yes-or-no answers boils down to seeing conversations as opportunities rather than obligations. Instead of shutting a dialogue down, just sprinkle in a little extra juice…share a thought (I haven't encountered food this unique at a party in a while; what do you think of these appetizers?), ask a question (Where did you find those unique earrings you're wearing? I love how bold they are!), or offer a small detail (You know, you're the second person to mention that show is great; I'll check it out).

If talking to strangers feels terrifying, imagine you're speaking to someone from your circle of safety, like your mom or a close friend. This mental shift helps soften your tone, ease your nerves, and make your responses more natural. The more you practice opening up, the more effortless conversations will become. Before we go further, please know I can hear some of you saying, "But Linda! I'm an introvert. I can't possibly do this!" Don't worry, I'm not here to turn you into someone you're not. While I'm going to gently pull you out of yourself so you can engage more confidently in conversation and strengthen your connection to the world around you, this isn't about abandoning your introvert status. It's about expanding your range. Mastering casual conversation doesn't mean becoming loud or extroverted; it means being able to show up as "yourself"... calm, observant, thoughtful, and still make meaningful contact with others. Think of it as adding a superpower to your existing tool kit, not replacing it. You don't have to be "on" all the time, just ready when it counts.

We all winced when Alex shut Jacob down with her blunt comment about her boring old chicken, but she could have had this man eating out of the palm of her hand if she had asked me what to do. First, she needed to tenderize her tone—it was sharp and could easily come across as dismissive. This wasn't about submitting to a man (or anyone) or being overly accommodating; it was about basic human courtesy. A warm but friendly tone, like the one you'd use when meeting your best friend's grandmother, signals approachability and respect, and that level of softness can open more doors than sharpness ever could. Her uninspired comment about the food didn't exactly indicate she was an interesting person to talk to either. I'd bet my right arm Jacob would have stayed by her side all night if Alex had used my easy formula. Here's how I'd like you to remember it when out and about—the Triple A.

THE TRIPLE A: ANSWER + ATTRIBUTE + ALSO

Question: "Do you recommend any entrées?"
Answer: "The chicken is good."
+
Attribute: "It's really *juicy* and roasted with rosemary and garlic." Feel free to place emphasis with sexy words.
+
Also: "By the way, the raw bar is fantastic. Do you like oysters, Jacob?"

Life does not owe you a warm, fuzzy blanket. If you are struggling with this barrier, you need to turn up the temperature on your life. Some of the deepest pain of being frozen solid comes from being too afraid to embrace new ideas and new things. Do you want to be trapped alone on a glacier while others are splashing around in the warmer waters where the real action is? It's not fun being cold, but feeling exposed to the elements is a natural and necessary part of growth and self-improvement. To be freed from this barrier you've got to face new experiences, learn new skills, expand your perspectives, and participate in your own existence! Oh, this makes you uncomfortable? There are no comfort zones, baby. Take a breath and remember discomfort is the driver that will push you to confront your fears, crack open that heart power zone, learn to listen with your entire body, and speak to people so they can see what a gem of a human being you are. And I guarantee you'll discover treasures in that discomfort if you're willing to look! Discomfort is often where our true potential, resilience, and creativity are hanging out, just waiting for us to grab on to them! Know that the discomfort you may feel is not a setback. It's a sign of progress that you're growing stronger and more confident in your ability to communicate. It's God's[2] way of telling you that you are breaking through this big barrier, pushing your boundaries, and moving forward in life to where the light is brightest, so you can feel warm. Aren't you excited to see how that feels? I know I am.

2. Now me, I'm a Jesus girl. But my methods are purely nondenominational, so know I respect your faith, whatever it may be.

***Now let me ask you this:***
***Do you get Botox injections?***

*I was once called in to help a celebrity client who was about to embark on a publicity tour for her upcoming book, but she needed some serious media coaching and wasn't happy with the person who was recommended to her. This woman was known for playing a "tough" role, and even though she was brilliant and beautiful, America was used to viewing her as a villain. Other coaches had worked with her, but she was still getting feedback that she was off-putting. As soon as I met her, I saw that her look and demeanor was indeed that of a villain—tense, rigid, and ready to go on the offensive. She may have thought she was projecting confidence, but instead she looked ready to attack. When I started the mock interview, she was easily triggered by questions—and her words became sharp and short as if we were engaging in verbal combat.*

*I gave her solutions so she could adjust her nonverbals to distance herself from the villain she was used to playing. She was going on a talk show where I knew there were always coffee mugs lined up perfectly on the table in front of the guest and the host. I told her that after she sat down, she should intentionally move the mug so that her heart power zone was fully visible to the audience, which also allowed her to put her hand near her heart area. I didn't want her to come off as aggressive like she did during our mock interview, so I taught her to slightly tilt her head as she began to answer questions using a soft tone. I also suggested she keep her hands above the desk with her palms exposed. Because your "package" is another tool that impacts the vibe you give off (we'll get to that later), I also told her it was important to wear softer colors and adjust her hairstyle to something looser. We had her NVC in shape within a matter of hours, but I had one final piece of advice for this gorgeous woman who had shed her severity. I looked her straight in the eye...my tone of voice was deadly serious..."Listen to me. Whatever you do, do not go get Botox. I know many Hollywood types get Botox regularly, but if you do this, you will undo everything we have just done."*

*By altering the natural expressions of your face, Botox can subtly diminish your emotional power. Our faces are deeply connected to how we experience and communicate emotions, both to ourselves and to others. The microexpressions that convey empathy, joy, sadness, or frustration are part of our emotional vocabulary. When Botox smooths those expressions, it can mute that vocabulary, creating a disconnection between how we feel inside and how we present those feelings outwardly. Since emotions are a profound source of personal power, guiding intuition, decision-making, and how we connect with others—limiting their expression can dull that inner strength by making a person look frozen.*

*Over time, this emotional detachment may not only affect how others perceive us, but how we perceive our-*

*selves as well, reducing the full impact of our authentic emotional energy. A blank face diminishes our power by stripping away the vital signals that convey emotions, intentions, and presence. Human connection and influence are deeply rooted in our ability to express emotions through facial expressions. A blank or expressionless face can create distance, making it harder for others to read our feelings or intentions, which weakens trust, rapport, and empathy. Without visible emotional cues, we lose a critical tool for commanding attention, fostering relationships, or asserting authority. A lack of expression can also reduce our own sense of emotional engagement, muting the feedback loop between feeling and expressing. In essence, our face becomes a mask that hides rather than amplifies our inner strength, diminishing our ability to fully project our personality and power into the world. Baby, it's your face, your decision, but think twice before you freeze up some of your power. And P.S., after all those successful television appearances, my client's book became a* New York Times *bestseller.*

## CHAPTER THREE

# Get Ahold of Yourself

Momma Bird used to wisely say, "Please do not bring your problems to my porch." Or, as I now like to say, "Please do not bring your problems to my party." It is not always appropriate for everyone to know, see, or hear everything that's going on with you! I do not want a big ole ball of issues bringing down my mood. If this sounds like you, would you please kindly keep your personal mess far away from my party? These messes show up in a few haphazard forms before a person even opens their mouth. Some people come off like a rogue tornado, debris flying everywhere...think Kramer from *Seinfeld,* sliding dramatically into Jerry's apartment without knocking, tripping over furniture, and blurting out all kinds of nonsense. Or Aubrey Plaza's character April on *Parks & Recreation*, with a permanent scowl planted on her face, her eyes shooting out laser beams of skepticism. Finally, we have Michael Scott, the misguided manager from *The Office*. His need for approval, love, and friendship is downright cringeworthy and drives a lot of his misguided decisions. I say this with love: If any of the above sounds at all like you, it's time for you to get it together. It doesn't have to be this way! Some of the smartest, most intelligent and interesting people I've met during my speaking and coaching career have battled these problems, but after making a few specific adjustments to their NVC, they now slide into a room as smoothly as fine pieces of silk.

Take Cassandra, aka "Miss Barely There," for example. You might not notice her right away—not because she isn't put-together, but because she carries herself like someone trying not to take up too much space. Cassandra is a real estate broker. She's smart, capable, warmhearted, and she genuinely wants to help people find their dream homes. She's well dressed in a chic pencil skirt, soft cashmere sweater, slingback heels, and tasteful makeup. On paper, she's got everything in place. But in person, something's off. Her posture tilts inward; her shoulders are slightly hunched as if she's bracing herself for rejection. Her smile flickers but doesn't quite land, and her eyes often drift downward when she speaks. There's a heaviness in the way she walks, like her confidence is dragging behind her, always a few steps out of reach.

She's dreamed of being a top broker ever since watching *House Hunters* in the nineties, and she works tirelessly…no breaks, no weekends off. So she doesn't understand why she's dead last in team sales. Determined to turn things around, Cassandra preps an open house with care: She lays out beautiful charcuterie platters, chills champagne, and tidies every corner of the space. But when the first guests arrive, she greets them softly, almost apologetically, and then quietly slips away to refill the brochure stack...*again*. When more couples arrive, she shares facts about the home in a low, slightly rushed voice, her hands fidgeting with the edge of her sweater. As more people file in, she approaches them reluctantly instead of offering a firm handshake and an energetic introduction with a big smile and a strong stance. Her nonverbals do not announce, "I'm in charge"—the woman comes off as an unwanted guest at her own open house! She forgets to invite people to enjoy the food or the view of the lake. It's not that she doesn't care; it's that she's so wrapped up in a sticky web of her own self-doubt that she forgets. Throughout the afternoon, potential buyers float through, curious about the house but not totally engaged in the experience, as Cassandra hasn't greeted them or shared any information. As she struggles on with the event, she stops trusting that her presence is enough to hold anyone's attention. Cassandra keeps drifting from room to room, present but not quite all there...almost like a ghost.

Mr. and Mrs. Interested spend nearly forty minutes exploring the home, clearly intrigued, but Cassandra never finds the nerve to check in with them beyond a few polite remarks, which leaves them with the impression she is incapable of getting a deal closed. They leave with a brochure and no real connection. Cassandra's face droops into sadness as she waves them off with a quiet "Thanks for coming," the tone of her voice managing to convey defeat—like she knows she'll never sell the place.

Later that week, the same couple tours homes with Ms. Competing Broker, who invites them to a quiet tea shop to chat about what they're looking for. She listens, asks questions, and exudes confidence and competence. Three weeks later, the couple closes on a beautiful Dutch colonial, and Ms. Competing Broker keeps the referrals rolling in. At the next sales meeting, Cassandra nearly chokes on her coffee when she sees Ms. Competing Broker's numbers—and the keys to her brand-new Mercedes convertible. Cassandra, kind and capable as she is, can't help but wonder: "Why can't I close a deal? Will I be driving my dad's ancient Corolla forever?" The truth is, it's not her knowledge or her effort that's holding her back. It's the quiet signal she sends with every bowed shoulder and uncertain glance—one that tells the world she doesn't believe in herself yet. And until she does, the world won't either.

Cassandra is frustrated and angry about her failure to increase her sales, and her immediate reaction is "I guess I just don't have what it takes." This attitude will ensure that Cassandra never sells so much as a broken-down garage. Every tool she needs to dominate at work is at her disposal, but her internal problems about not believing she can be a great salesperson are presenting front and center in her body language, keeping her from crossing the finish line. All her personal, negative inner messaging pours out, making an otherwise capable woman appear timid, inexperienced, and barely visible. Her fear was so palpable in her NVC that no one took her seriously. She had an entire house full of potential buyers, and while she might have seemed kind, the mousey vibe displayed in her NVC made everyone feel like she didn't want to be bothered (if they noticed her at all). No wonder her competitor is driving a Mercedes and she's in that old wreck.

## BARRIER #2: FLOODING

> ***Flooding***: *Individuals whose nonverbal cues, movements, and verbal expressions reveal more information than a person intended, sometimes beyond what's considered socially appropriate. It can also result in a person unknowingly sharing inner emotions, anxieties, and experiences that would be better kept private. This can cause mixed signals, create distance between people, and result in self-sabotage.*
>
> ***The tired, old excuse:*** *"I'm an emotional person; what's the big deal?"*

Bless people who have no awareness of how their inner thoughts, feelings, and anxieties are pouring out all over the place, creating a big sloppy (and unnecessary) mess. There is a war being waged within them all, and the mission of the war is clear: Let's keep this person from getting anything they want. Flooding can create a quiet chaos in people's lives, as it exposes more than they intended—sometimes far more. When someone's body language, tone, or expression is bursting forth with a tsunami of private emotions or experiences, it can send confusing or overwhelming signals to others. What was meant to stay internal pours out, and the result is often discomfort or misinterpretation. People may pull away, unsure how to respond, or they may view the person as unstable or too intense. Who wouldn't run fast if they found themselves in the path of a tsunami? In relationships, this can create emotional distance instead of closeness. In professional settings, it can undermine credibility. Over time, this involuntary but intense type of inadvertent oversharing becomes a form of self-sabotage, eroding trust, confidence, and connection. The worst part is, these people don't know that their flooding is so unappealing it makes it harder for them to reach goals or forge connections with anyone. The insidious dark waters seeping out of them will eventually wear them down until they feel like a rotting old pier—about to collapse into the ocean in a pile of broken pieces.

Case in point, let's talk about my buddy Derek. Derek was determined to get his dream job and was giving the interview his all. Derek sat across from the hiring manager, his knee bouncing so violently it rattled the table. He leaned forward, *way too far forward*, giving the impression he was about to hop across the table and into the interviewer's lap. He nodded aggressively at every word like he was a little puppy begging for a treat. Derek's forced smile stretched a little too wide, coming off as false…and, frankly, creepy. "I just really love this company," he blurted out while the woman was trying to ask him a question. When he did speak at the appropriate moments, his voice was a notch too eager—sounding higher pitched than usual and with a faster than normal cadence. His hands gripped the armrests of his chair like he was on a plane that was about to go down. Then, in a snap, they'd be flailing around as he spoke, palms open, but in an exaggerated attempt at warmth that fell flat.

When asked about his work experience, he answered too quickly, his words spilling out like he was at the Oscars and was afraid he'd be cut off before he thanked everyone. Then he added, "I'll do anything. Seriously, anything." As he said this he leaned forward even farther, upping the creep factor even higher. It didn't help that he punctuated this statement with a nervous, high-pitched chuckle. The interviewer offered a polite smile but pushed her chair back as far as she could, wanting to stay clear of the river of desperation oozing out of Derek—the jittery posture, darting eye contact, and overeager interruptions. As they shook hands at the end, he gripped just a little too tightly, holding on a beat too long. "I really hope to hear from you soon," he said, his voice borderline pleading.

I'm sure you can guess that Derek did not get the job. Who wants to be around all that buzzing energy from nine to five every day? Can you imagine this guy on a date? Nope, because you'd run out of the restaurant. Eventually, exhaustion will force people like Cassandra and Derek to surrender to the LIE that they aren't worthy, all is lost, and it's time to give up. Can you imagine an uglier battle? It's a nonsensical behavior that we've got to get rid of, *especially* when we're eager to be successful. Coming off as needy through your nonverbal communication like Derek, with the excessive leaning in, lack of personal space, anxious fidgeting, or overly eager facial expressions, can unintentionally push people away in all areas of life rather than draw them to you.

These behaviors are like a bat signal for insecurity or a lack of self-sufficiency, which research shows can reduce not only your attractiveness but also your social value. A study published in 2024 in the *Archives of Sexual Behavior* found that individuals perceived as overly dependent or emotionally clingy were rated as less desirable partners. Nonverbal cues that convey neediness can also trigger discomfort or a sense of obligation in others, making interactions feel emotionally draining or imbalanced.

## LET'S FACE IT, ERASE IT, AND REPLACE IT

For classic flooders like Cassandra and Derek, they've got to clear out their "emotional attic" to fix the flood that's causing them problems. Over the years, unresolved feelings like anger, guilt, sadness, insecurity, shame, and fear can accumulate just as dust gathers in an abandoned space. When we feel rejected, unseen, or unworthy, it's easy to push these painful emotions aside, hoping that "out of sight, out of mind" will make them disappear. However, our minds do not work that way. Unprocessed emotions will eventually build up and burst open, causing unexpected disruptions in our lives. The stored-away emotions are far from inert—they seep out when we least expect it like pus slowly oozing out of an infected wound, only to grow stronger until they are impossible to ignore.

Have you ever watched a movie and been surprised to

find you're crying? That's a tiny hurt announcing itself, telling you *it wants out.* The more we avoid confronting these emotions, the more they accumulate and take up valuable mental space. Eventually, your mind is as messed up as an episode of *Hoarders*—you can't get clarity or move toward your purpose. Recognizing this leakage is the essential first step toward healing and bringing forth the successful and in-control version of yourself.

A powerful method to address this buildup is what I call "the Express and Release" process. It begins by acknowledging and identifying your emotions. Take the time to reflect on the events that have hurt you, asking yourself why you feel the way you do. Sometimes, speaking with a trusted friend, mentor, pastor, or therapist can provide the clarity needed to understand the truth behind your emotions. This mentor doesn't have to be a formal figure; they can be an emotional ally who holds you accountable as you navigate through your feelings.

For example, chances are Lydia would not be the successful graphic designer she is today without the help of a kindly and supportive manager early in her career. Lydia's flooding was an especially nasty variety, so forceful that once unleashed it threatened to wipe out everything in her path. At times Lydia would walk into her manager's office and begin to stomp her feet like a child. Red-faced and crying so hard she could barely get the words out, she'd finally blurt between sobs, "I'm being undermined!" These tantrums erupted after being asked to do a small task by the Big Boss, like run out and get him a coffee or pick up a gift for his kid's birthday.

After Lydia had done this several times, her manager finally had enough of such childish (and unprofessional) behavior. "Lydia, shut the door. Now." As soon as they had privacy, Lydia's manager set her straight: "You cannot act this way if you want to work here—or anywhere. I know how talented you are, and I pushed to get you hired here, but now you're having a fit over being asked to go on a coffee run? You need to get yourself together and find out what's behind this. By the way, Big Boss has mentioned to me how annoyed and angry you look when he asks you to do something."

At first, Lydia wasn't sure why she was acting like an angry kindergartner; she was smart and a hard worker and didn't want to exhibit such embarrassing behavior. She appreciated her manager's bluntness (and not firing her) and vowed to get a deeper understanding of what was setting her off and promised it would never happen again.

Lydia spent the weekend in a state of self-reflection, thinking long and hard about why these basic requests set her off in such a crazy fashion. Eventually she realized she was being triggered by a frustrating pattern she witnessed growing up. Raised by a single mother who worked in an insurance office, Lydia recalled how her mother (the only woman in the office) was automatically expected to do tasks like making coffee, taking notes, and running errands even though she was a top producer. The men in the office were only expected to make sales, and they were rewarded with bonuses and promotions as a result. Her mother never got her due. She was never promoted, rarely got raises, and they struggled as a result. Lydia's anger about this unfair treatment was combined with a narrative that existed only in her head—that she'd end up the same way. After a deeply sincere apology to her manager, Lydia was able to get a handle on this issue by reminding herself her mother's story was not her own. Getting a coffee for her boss, in her case, did not mean she was destined to a lifetime of struggle and unfairness. Lydia began meditating, exercising more, and practicing gratitude to help keep the floodwaters at bay.

Once you have identified your flood-inducing emotions, allow yourself to feel and validate them. Don't shy away from those dark, musty feelings that have been tucked away in your emotional attic. Permit yourself to experience the pain without judgment. By fully embracing your emotions, you diminish their power and make plenty of room for positive emotions like confidence and self-worth.

Finally, it's important to process and release these feelings in a healthy way. Whether through conversation, prayer, journaling, art, or physical activity, find a method that helps you channel your emotions constructively. When you make a conscious effort to process these feelings, you prevent them from seeping out uncontrollably and creating chaos in your life. Remember, an occasional flood is a natural part of being human. When you're in the thick of intense feelings, try not to be overly critical of yourself afterward. Instead, take a moment to reflect on how you might respond differently in the future. Consider the person you aspire to be and make choices that align with that vision. In doing so, you determine the kind of emotional legacy you leave behind.

Cleaning out your emotional attic isn't just about letting go; it's about creating space for the new positive experiences and relationships you want to have. Embrace the process and watch as the clutter clears away to reveal a brighter, more authentic you. And baby, it's not going to happen overnight. This is work. But God gave you emotions, and they aren't anything you can't handle...but never let them drive the car. You are in charge.

When you walk away from a situation feeling like your nonverbal behavior didn't reflect your worth, it can be disheartening, but it's also an invitation to continually reflect on the things your body remembers but your mind might try to forget. So, the most powerful thing you can do when this happens is explore the beliefs underneath: Do you feel safe being seen? Do you believe you have to earn your place in the room? Are you afraid that being fully yourself might lead to disapproval or abandonment? Are you still trying to protect a younger version of yourself who learned to stay small to survive? Keep at it with the journaling, therapy, or even just honest inner dialogue so you can untangle these patterns. When you address these root causes, your presence begins to shift naturally...not because you're forcing it, but because you're no longer carrying the weight that distorted it in the first place.

The truth is, not all floods are instantly and permanently fixed, so I like to tell my clients, "Pause for the cause!" What's the cause? Your dignity, reputation, self-worth, and ability to succeed on the highest level. It's crucial to prevent your personal floodwaters from getting in the way of what you want. Even as you're putting in the work and cleaning that attic, sometimes feelings bubble up. You do not want them to escalate and find yourself so over the top with your behavior at a job interview that you're like a five-year-old high on sugar. Think of Derek, practically sitting in the interviewer's lap, literally begging for a job. This behavior will not do! I have an easy exercise that I recommend doing when you feel that pulse racing and you are eager for an opportunity. Before you start flying around the room or running your mouth, you need to pause for the cause and just **SIT.**

### SIT

Stop.
*Halt any immediate reaction and take a mental break.*

Inhale.
*Take a deep breath to reset your nervous system.*

Think.
*Reflect on the situation and your response before acting.*

The idea is that by taking a pause and a few deep breaths, you create space between the emotional reaction and your behaviors. This simple exercise helps ground you in the present moment, allowing you to reflect on the situation and release any negativity that's brewing inside you. Save yourself the trouble of looking out of control, baby! Keep SIT in your tool kit.

The key for folks like Cassandra and Derek is to know thyself! This is why I want you to start keenly observing how you are operating and feeling in different situations *today*.

When is it that you feel most comfortable in your skin? When do you sense people feel most comfortable with you? Think about your triggers of discomfort. If you are dating, is there a specific period during the date when you feel the least comfortable? Do you need a warm-up to access your true self before meeting a date? If so, access your emotional attic and think about why. When is it that your dates or spouse seem like they're enjoying their time with you? What is your body doing to elicit that reaction? If you're swirling around in negative, upsetting energy with a spouse or date...what is your body saying to them in that instance?

Sometimes a simple facial expression can cause some of our biggest communication mishaps. If you find that people often misinterpret your mood, think you're upset when you're not, or avoid approaching you, it might be worth considering how your neutral expression is perceived. In professional or social settings, your nonverbals play a huge role in how others relate to you, and an unintentional "Resting Bitch Face" can send signals that contradict your true intentions or emotions, potentially hindering your ability to build connections or work collaboratively. If you notice that people often give you odd looks or seem constantly surprised by your words and desires, it could be a sign that you need to perk up that face.

At the weekly wine club, Margaret's face just would not cooperate—it was completely out of sync with what she was actually feeling, and she had no idea. As she swirled a beautiful jewel-colored pinot noir, her nose wrinkled involuntarily, her upper lip curling as if she'd just licked a battery. "Oh wow, this is…lovely," she said, nodding too enthusiastically, which added to the impression that she was pretending to like it. The sommelier raised an eyebrow. She actually *did* like it—smooth, oaky, just the right amount of spice—but her facial expression suggested she was swallowing vinegar. It wasn't just the bad and mediocre wines she sampled that betrayed her either. Even when a buttery chardonnay delighted her palate, her eyes narrowed like she was solving a crime. Margaret was deflated when the hostess poured out the rest of the bottle into everyone else's glass, skipping hers. She really wanted a bit more of that delicious chardonnay. When Margaret asked why she didn't get any, she got an awkward apology. "Oh, sorry, miss. Your reaction made me think you hated it." A silence filled the room as the other members stole glances at each other, whispering, trying to decide whether Margaret was secretly the club's toughest critic or just deeply unhinged. "Hated it?" Margaret said. "That chardonnay tasted like sunshine itself!" Margaret has got herself a case of the dreaded resting bitch face, aka RBF.

Resting bitch face is a pop culture term used to describe a neutral facial expression that unintentionally appears angry, annoyed, or unapproachable. It's not about someone actually feeling those emotions—it's about how their face is perceived when they're simply at rest. Research published in the journal *Trends in Cognitive Sciences* and further studied by behavioral researchers Jason Rogers and Abbe Macbeth has shown that people with RBF tend to display subtle traces of contempt in their neutral expressions—such as a slight tightening around the eyes or mouth, which others subconsciously interpret as negative.

Resting bitch face isn't limited to regular folk; several gorgeous celebrities have been labeled, often unfairly, as having resting bitch face. Kristen Stewart has been frequently called out for her serious, unsmiling expressions in public, and she has addressed comments about her perceived lack of facial emotion publicly. In a 2015 conversation with *Elle UK*, she stated, "The whole smiling thing is weird because I actually smile a lot. I literally want to be like, Dude, you would think I was cool if you got to know me." That same year, in a 2015 interview with MTV News, Stewart recounted director Woody Allen asking about her neutral expression during filming, noting, "He actually used the word resting."

Victoria Beckham, known for rarely smiling in photos, has embraced the image. Responding to a question in a *Vogue* interview about why she doesn't smile, she replied, "I'm smiling on the inside."

Anna Kendrick has used her humor to address perceptions of her neutral facial expression. In a 2014 tweet, she wrote, "Is there a filter on Instagram that fixes Bitchy Resting Face? I'm asking for a friend." During a 2015 appearance on *The Late Late Show with James Corden*, Kendrick discussed her so-called resting bitch face with fellow guests Brittany Snow and Hailee Steinfeld. She expressed frustration about being perceived as intimidating or upset when she's simply at rest, leading to a lighthearted conversation about the challenges of misinterpreted facial expressions. So, if you have this issue, consider yourself in good company.

But the truth is, resting bitch face can lead to unfair judgments, social misunderstandings, or people keeping their distance without ever getting to know the person behind the expression. While the term is often used humorously, it reflects a deeper truth about how quickly and unconsciously we form impressions based on facial cues, and how easily those impressions can be misleading. However, I ask you to hear this: *Having so-called resting bitch face is not your fault.* It is a stigma that has been put on women, especially Black women, and this is a heavy weight for my sisters to hold.

You've probably been there—you're just waiting for the bus or standing in line at the store like everyone else, thinking about your to-do list when someone opens their mouth to say, "You look mean, unhappy, or even worse…sad." Resting bitch face isn't a joke; it can really feel like an attack on women. I know none of your male friends have been complaining about this problem, am I right?

So, before I give you my tips for putting your best face forward if you want to appear more approachable…remember this: Your face is perfect. Ignore the haters. Love the seriousness behind your beauty! You are gorgeous, your skin is flawless, and every feature on your face is a unique work of art. And that person who has the audacity to think you look like a B*&$%? That person is probably just uncomfortable with themselves. Have you ever considered that they are the real B*&$%? Maybe the best thing for your face would be for this joker to go jump in a lake, because he has no idea how much is on your mind—taking care of family and friends, earning money, running your company, managing your team, keeping toned with Pilates, keeping your hair and nails on point, being present in your new relationship with a hot guy. In fact, if you're thinking about all that, and making all of that happen for yourself, that sounds more like "Resting Boss Face" to me. We all know being a boss is a lot of work, so no wonder a less than perfectly approachable facial expression lands there from time to time!

I get approached by women all the time (never men, by the way) about resting boss face. When they ask me what can be done about it, I ask them to pull out their cell phone and show me a picture of their "best face forward." When they show me a vacation picture or a new headshot I'll ask, "What was your emotional state in that moment?" A positive story always follows.

When someone asks if you're okay at work, or your girlfriend pulls you aside and points out your RBF and supposed negative thinking, does your response reflect that you are agitated, upset, overwhelmed, or feeling pressured or undervalued? Or is your response "I'm not thinking anything negative; I'm just thinking! Period." If the latter is usually the case, know that you're not the first person to experience this disconnect.

A resting boss face can definitely show up when you're just thinking. In fact, it often does. When you're deep in thought, your face naturally shifts into a neutral or focused expression, and without realizing it, your features might tighten, your brow may furrow slightly, or your mouth might press into a line—all of which can unintentionally signal annoyance, disapproval, or even arrogance to others. But in reality, you might just be concentrating, processing, or lost in your own world. Because thinking is an internal process, we're not always aware of how we're coming across externally. This is one reason why a resting boss face tends to be misread so often: People assume the expression reflects a mood or attitude, when it's really just a by-product of being mentally engaged or introspective.

There are many other moments when a neutral or focused expression is mistaken for resting boss face, even though the person isn't feeling irritated at all. For instance, when someone is tired, their facial muscles naturally relax or droop, which can make them appear disinterested or grumpy. In loud or overstimulating environments, people may seem tense or withdrawn simply because they're overwhelmed, not because they're unfriendly. Shyness or social anxiety can also lead to a closed-off expression that reads as aloof, when in reality the person is feeling vulnerable or unsure. Facial structure plays a role too. Some people naturally have features like downturned lips or low brows that unintentionally convey displeasure. Others may be lost in thought, replaying a conversation, problem-solving, or managing inner dialogue, which can create an intense or unreadable expression. Even physical discomfort, like a headache or stiff posture, can subtly show on the face in ways others misinterpret. In short, what gets labeled as RBF is often just a moment of being human, misread through a limited lens.

If you are concerned about resting boss face, just know that the more intense the emotion you are experiencing, the longer you tend to hold on to that feeling. This means your face is locked into that specific position, fueled by the emotion, until you change your emotional state and release it. Let me ask you this: How many times has a girlfriend said to you, "Girl, fix your face"?

Do I think we have to walk around smiling nonstop? No, nonstop smiling is not natural (especially if you're a boss). I choose to look at it this way: How do you want to be perceived? Do you want to be a people magnet or a people repellent? You can't control how everyone will perceive you, but you can control and manage your emotions and how they visibly appear. In other words, as Momma Bird used to say, "Chil', whatever you've got cooking up in that mind does matter because it's served on the platter that's your face."

For women in leadership positions or who aspire to move up in our careers, it's important to remember that our facial expressions are contagious and can affect others. This is called "Emotional Contagion." Emotional contagion is the process by which people "catch" and absorb the emotions of those around them, often without realizing it. This happens through facial expressions but can also be transmitted by tone of voice, posture, and energy. One person's mood can ripple outward and influence others, spreading joy, anxiety, anger, or sadness like an emotional virus.

Think of the woman in the office who always appears to be angry or upset about something. Look at her forehead, which is the social landscape of the face, as that's where we use our eyes and eyebrows to connect with others. You will notice in the resting position of her forehead that there are two lines etched in the glabella, the skin between the eyebrows and above the nose. This is an indication of someone who is quick to anger. The etched lines are visible because those muscles are used constantly, powered by the emotions. It's a natural part of human connection, driven by empathy and mirror neurons, but it can also be overwhelming or disruptive when the emotions being absorbed are intense or negative.

I was patient zero of an emotional contagion shortly after my mother died. I was working in sales at the time and stopped by the office to pick up a few things. When someone on my team saw the look of sadness on my face, he immediately picked up the emotion. After he shared the news that my mother had passed with the rest of the team, the dark emotion spread; everyone caught the sadness, the grief, and the sense of overwhelm—and ultimately no one was in the right frame of mind to be closing deals. The emotional contagion resulted in a bad sales day. Obviously, life throws us emotional challenges that we have no control over, such as a loved one's passing. However, as leaders we need to remember that humans have the spontaneous tendency to synchronize facial expressions with others, so being mindful of what you're spreading around will have a direct impact on your entire team, and possibly your bottom line.

If you can relate to Margaret, whose facial expression gave off the wrong impression at the wine club, don't freak out. Once you've recognized the problem, you can work on adjusting your expression through deliberate practice to reveal an irresistible face that gets attention. First, you need to get to know *your own* personal RBF. Recruit a trusted sister who will tell you the honest-to-God truth—do NOT recruit your mother or a friend who always agrees with you. Ask the trusted sister to describe what happens to your face when it wanders into RBF territory. You need to know exactly what your eyes, eyebrows, forehead, jaw, and mouth are doing.

It also helps to be aware of the type of situations that cause an RBF flare-up. Know your triggers! For example, maybe Margaret the wine sipper is new to the group and feels self-conscious in situations where she doesn't know everyone. Your RBF may be unleashed at work meetings because deep down you worry your boss won't like your work even though you are properly prepared with a great new idea and are extremely excited about the project. When you know your triggers, you can plan to take a moment to consciously relax your face when you are about to enter such a situation.

Another simple technique for eliminating RBF involves using gentle biofeedback cues. Biofeedback cues are the subtle internal or external signals that help you become more aware of what your body is doing so you can consciously adjust it. When you feel the sensation of physical tension creeping into your body, you tend to notice it in other parts of the body, such as the neck or shoulders. We don't often think about how our facial muscles feel, which is why biofeedback can help us be aware when they're tensing up.

Identifying facial muscle tension starts with developing a habit of checking in with your body throughout the day, searching for those signals. Tension often accumulates in areas like the jaw, forehead, or around the eyes without us realizing it, especially during stress, deep focus, or emotional discomfort. One easy technique is to periodically pause and ask yourself: "What is my face doing right now?" You might notice a tight jaw, furrowed brow, or shallow breathing, all of which can act as a signal that tension is building in your face. Sometimes catching your reflection in a mirror or window can reveal an expression you weren't aware of, like a scowl or a blank stare. Emotional shifts, like feeling anxious, irritated, or overstimulated, can also serve as cues to pause and check in with your face. Even recurring situations that involve concentration, like reading emails or sitting in traffic, can become pattern-based signals that it's time to soften your expression and take a deeper breath. By tuning in to these subtle indicators, you can develop greater physical awareness and emotional control over time.

Let these moments of awareness prompt you to consciously relax your muscles. Softening your eyes, unclenching your jaw, and slightly parting your lips can help reset your expression and, even better, reduce overall tension. With regular practice, you will learn *to feel* those physical signs you toss out. You'll become instantly aware when you feel your mouth moving into a frown or your jaw clenching. Over time, awareness and small adjustments will reshape your natural expression into one that aligns more closely with how you truly feel. Embracing these changes not only improves how others perceive you but can also enhance your own mood and social interactions.

Once you've established awareness, it's only a matter of replacing that tension with positive expressions. You can start by engaging your eyes: Eye contact is one of the most powerful tools for softening your expression and making you seem more approachable. Let your eyes "smile" by slightly widening them or showing warmth when you look at others.

Smiling with the eyes, often referred to as a "Duchenne smile," positively influences how a person is perceived. A Duchenne smile is a genuine, heartfelt smile that engages both the mouth and the eyes. Named after nineteenth-century French neurologist Guillaume Duchenne de Boulogne, this type of smile is characterized by the upturned corners of the mouth *and* the activation of the muscles around the eyes, specifically the orbicularis oculi, which causes the eyes to crinkle or "smile." Duchenne identified that only true emotional joy activates both regions. Unlike polite or forced smiles, which typically involve just the mouth, a Duchenne smile is often seen as a reliable indicator of authentic happiness. This type of smile is widely recognized as more genuine and warmer compared to a non-Duchenne or "polite" smile, which involves only the mouth.

Studies have shown that people who display Duchenne smiles are often perceived as more trustworthy, likable, and competent. For instance, research published in the journal *Psychological Science* found that observers were better at detecting genuine emotions when facial expressions involved the eyes. Other research has shown that genuine smiles, especially those engaging the eyes, can even predict long-term personal and professional success because they communicate authenticity and warmth. Julia Roberts, Jennifer Aniston, and the late actor Robin Williams all exhibit classic Duchenne smiles.

Curiously enough, a true Duchenne smile can't easily be faked with muscle control alone; it tends to appear naturally when you feel authentic warmth, amusement, or joy. This is another instance where imagining something pleasant is actually one of the most effective ways to create a genuine smile that includes your eyes. Start by thinking of something that makes you genuinely happy: a funny memory, a loved one's face, a favorite place; or imagine that cute puppy again. Let yourself linger in that moment just long enough to feel a soft emotional shift. As you do, you'll likely notice a natural upward pull at the corners of your mouth *and* a gentle crinkling around your eyes. Your cheeks may lift slightly, and the muscles around your eyes will engage subtly...this is the hallmark of a smile that feels authentic to others. When I first started studying nonverbal communication I practiced in front of a mirror. First, try a polite, social smile with just your mouth, then shift to smiling while thinking of something that warms your heart. The difference will be noticeable. Not just in your appearance, but in how you feel too.

Understanding how your facial expressions are interpreted—like Margaret's unintentional scowl, Cassandra's shrinking presence, or Derek's over-the-top desperation—is just one part of a much bigger story. At the core of each of these communication breakdowns is flooding, the messy emotional spillover that happens when we haven't fully processed what's going on beneath the surface. Cassandra didn't need more polish; she needed to believe she belonged in the room. Derek didn't need to be more enthusiastic; he needed to trust that he was enough without the performance. Their bodies betrayed them not because they were broken, but because unspoken fears and insecurities had been running the show for too long.

But here's what I really want you to know: Once you learn to recognize the flood is coming, you can dam it up before everything overflows. Once you see how your internal narratives shape your nonverbal communication, you can begin to shift them. You can clean out the emotional attic, release the weight you've been carrying, and show up in a way that aligns with the powerful, capable, magnetic person you already are. You'll know the power that comes from managing your energy, regulating your expression, and walking into every room with your presence rooted in truth—not fear. Whether you've been hiding like Cassandra, overreaching like Derek, or misread like Margaret, you're not stuck. You are in the process of becoming the clearest, calmest, most impactful version of yourself. And that version? That version gets noticed, gets heard, and gets results.

***Let me ask you this: Can you tell the difference between awkwardness and an honest-to-God jerk by looking at his face?***

*Sometimes life throws a real live jerk in front of us, and the sad truth is that this is not always a NVC problem. You need to be able to identify the real thing, because I don't want you wasting a single second on an honest-to-God jerk. The true jerk has three distinct expressions that serve as his signature: contempt, the eye roll, and the mocking brow. Contempt is the silent message in his gaze, a subtle signal that others are unworthy of his attention. This condescending attitude finds its perfect punctuation in an eye roll—a swift, almost reflexive motion that dismisses opinions as trivial and ideas as beneath him. Dominating the ensemble, the mocking brow arches in a perpetual display of superiority, transforming even a fleeting smile into a tool of derision. Together, these expressions create a visual language of scorn, clearly revealing his disrespectful nature and the toxic pride that drives his every interaction. Stay far away.*

## CHAPTER FOUR

# Don't Just Stand There

At every gathering, there's always someone who seems to vanish into the background. Have you ever wanted to do this? Unsure of how to jump into the flow of conversation, you just linger on the sidelines, and your silence is louder than anything you might have said if you had the courage to speak up. The hum of other people's chatter and laughter only stirs up panic, leaving you standing awkwardly, fidgeting with your clothes, and looking around for the nearest exit. Despite your desire to be part of the action, each moment of hesitation reinforces the feeling of isolation, turning what could be a good time into an exercise in misery. Know that I see your pain! It's terrible to be out in the world when you are paralyzed by uncertainty, or unsure of how to behave or what to say. As the awkwardness builds, the natural inclination to retreat into yourself only gets deeper, rendering you unable to make small talk or engage in any meaningful way. You stand there, unsure of what's expected, scanning the room like an observer rather than a participant.

Your silence is not from a lack of desire to join in, but from not having clarity about *where* you fit. A stream of self-doubt continually runs through your mind, making simple interactions feel like insurmountable challenges. You are stuck in limbo, a place where you do nothing because you are afraid of saying or doing the wrong thing. This is a painful place to be, but I'm going to be real with you. Baby, this kind of behavior is sad, pathetic, and keeping you away from so many of life's blessings! It's time to get to the root of it all so you can permanently delete your presocializing terrors.

The quinceañera was a joyous, lively event, and everyone was having a good time dancing and enjoying the good food—except for one small group of people who had isolated themselves. In the farthest corner of the reception hall, a cluster of misfits huddled together in a circle as far away from the action of the party as possible. One man fiddled anxiously with his champagne glass, his shoulders hunched sadly inward. A woman with stiff posture nodded excessively at a joke, her awkward chuckle vanishing into the background noise. Another guest, arms crossed tightly over her chest, shifted uncomfortably whenever a stranger passed too close, her body angled protectively toward the group as if they shared an unspoken agreement: They were safer together. They sipped their drinks slowly, eyes darting toward the dance floor with the same mix of longing and dread, knowing they would not dare step into the current of confident, effortless revelers. Instead, even as the sound of Bad Bunny filled the room, pulling most of the guests to the dance floor, these folks remained tethered to their corner.

I call these people "Lifeboaters" because they cling to one another like survivors of a shipwreck, trapped in an imaginary lifeboat of their own making...an awkward solidarity in a sea of celebration. You see the lifeboaters at every party and social event, and maybe you feel magnetically drawn to this solitary group of like-minded citizens. Lifeboaters are masterful when it comes to finding their own dark, dank corner, creating a space that guarantees no one will talk to them. The energy these people emit is dull and stale as a flat soda. There's no sizzle! No satisfying crispness or bubbliness whatsoever in the personalities they are portraying publicly. Could anyone sound less appealing to talk to? At every party they manage to exude the energy of passengers on the *Titanic* who know the ship is about to go down. Why all the fear? I'm not kidding; sometimes I see these folks bonded together at an event and they haven't even bothered to take their coats off! C'mon! Are y'all staying or going?

## BARRIER #3: FLAT

> ***Flat:*** *When fear and discomfort prevent people from being able to integrate into a group conversation or activity. Instead of actively engaging, they default to lingering in the background, often huddled in corners with others who share their hesitation. They become part of an invisible cluster, physically present but socially absent, not able to add the slightest ripple to conversations with any outsiders.*

***The tired, old excuse:*** *"There's nothing wrong with me; I'm just a bit introverted."*

People suffering from this barrier drain the energy from a space by passively existing rather than participating. They often consider themselves neutral, but their passivity has the opposite effect…it's subtly repellent. They may not realize it, but they are actually snubbing every single person at the event! You've got to learn to engage, speak, enjoy those passed appetizers, and share the specialness you have to offer with other guests. Otherwise, you can look forward to being as forgettable as a drink that's lost its fizz: technically there, but leaving people wanting something more satisfying. Let's take a look at how other folks drain the vibe with their flatness.

Monica is what I call a classic "Lurker." Lurkers are the quiet shadows who hang out at the edge of group conversations but never manage to penetrate the circle. Monica drifts through the botanic garden's annual fundraiser like a ghost. She feels like a princess in her carefully selected formal gown from Runway, but she might as well be Cinderella pretransformation. She behaves as if she doesn't deserve to be part of the conversation, so she lingers on the fringes in what I call "the Zone of Safety." Monica hovers just outside of a lively group of people, but she never steps into the circle. Instead of actively engaging, she resorts to shallow nods and half-hearted laughter at jokes she wasn't a part of, hoping proximity alone will count as participation. But no one truly acknowledges her, other than to notice someone is just skulking around the group awkwardly.

She confines herself to the zone of safety, fooling herself into thinking she's socializing, but it's just an illusion. With a drink in hand and a gaze that flickers just past eye contact, lurkers like Monica drift from group to group, close enough to hear fragments of stories, but always a step removed. They're not shy, exactly, but more like an observer playing a game of proximity, drawn to connection yet hesitant to break the surface. While others dive into the noise and heat of social exchange, the lurker lingers in the cool margins. Monica keeps enough distance that it's highly unlikely anyone will ask her a question or engage with her directly. Her body is angled slightly away, as if she might bolt at any moment.

Her feet are expressing a nonverbal communication that speaks volumes: When a person does not want to be where they are, their feet will automatically point toward the nearest exit. Look down at your feet the next time you're trapped in a conversation with a pushy PTA mom or a dull man who won't stop talking—I promise you they'll be aimed toward the door. To the people actually involved, Monica is barely there. She's just a faint, awkward presence on the outskirts. Occasionally, she shifts from one group to another, a drifter searching half-heartedly at best for some island to settle on. The more she moves and hovers, the more she seems out of place, neither fully inside nor outside, just trapped in a pathetic limbo, waiting for a moment of connection that will never arrive.

Being flat will have you spinning in a whirlwind of negativity that's so powerful you will never escape it. In fact, it's likely you *believe* you don't belong in the action because you've strongly identified yourself as a quiet introvert. You swear you don't care so much either, so you've found every excuse in the book to remain flat, and therefore always on the periphery of life. This barrier fosters a chronic inability to engage with the outside world. Being flat is so all-encompassing that if you don't face it head-on, eventually, you won't even bother trying to connect with others at all. Until you get yourself sorted out, you can expect social isolation, stalled career and personal growth, and an intense sense of loneliness and helplessness. So, unless you want the most important relationship in your life to be with your sofa, it's time to make some changes. Let's get you movin' and shakin', baby!

## LET'S FACE IT, ERASE IT, AND REPLACE IT

You can overcome your social invisibility and finally be seen with my technique, EASE. Whether you identify as a lifeboater who searches out other flat people at events and clings to them as if your life depends on it, or you are a lurker, hovering around other people's conversations all by yourself, my prescription for navigating a social event or any other interaction will get you over this barrier. Going forward, you will make an impact with your interactions, and I dare say you'll learn to enjoy yourself in the process. No more dark corners or zone of safety for you. Your sad group huddle in the corner, or awkward, silent sideliner days are about to be behind you. From now on, you will step into a room with presence and purpose.

My first words of advice: Do not let yourself overthink an entrance! You're not launching yourself to Mars! Confidence isn't about forcing a performance; you just need to trust yourself in the present moment. Anytime you feel alone, odd, or like a pariah at an event, remind yourself that those negative feelings are part of your past. Don't risk dragging that hesitation along with you. Instead, get excited about giving your life a fresh narrative and walk in as if you belong, *because you do.* Stand tall, take a breath, and move with ease. Become curious about the moment, the people, and what's happening around you. Presence isn't about perfection; it's about being fully where you are. My four-part process EASE, which is an acronym for **e**nter with presence, **a**dapt to the energy of the room, **s**ituate yourself strategically, and **e**ngage in conversation, will serve as your road map for successfully navigating social events.

The way you physically **ENTER** a space sets the tone for how people perceive you. If you're sneaking in unnoticed and then scurry into your little mouse hole, your impact in the space is zero. It doesn't get much sadder than that. I want you to use these simple NVC skills to walk into any room and turn heads. Think Idris Elba. Honey, when that man walks, we all lookin'. You don't have to be a sex pot or Idris to pull off a good walk. At a basic level, make sure you always stand tall, keep your heart power zone open by holding your shoulders back and allowing your chest to be open, and make brief eye contact with people in the room.

I'll stress this: LOOK at people. Even when you're on the way to the coat check. Even when you're just entering Starbucks for a quick espresso shot. Look people in the eye so you make that impression. Speaking of impressions, the actor Matthew Broderick, who has been with his wife, Sarah Jessica Parker, for thirty years, told Andy Cohen, the host of *Watch What Happens Live*, that it was her walk that hooked him. "I saw her walking down the street and thought, that's it." Your walk isn't just a means of getting from one place to another; it's a representation of your personality and style. Let your body communicate confidence as you move, even if you don't feel it yet. When you walk around like you own the world, people will step aside.

I know letting go of your old ways and making an entrance takes courage, but trust Auntie Linda on this one. In a now legendary social psychology experiment conducted in 1975 at Columbia University, researchers tested how far someone could get by simply *acting like they belonged*. They had people walk into movie theaters, college dorms, and even office buildings without permission and found that about 70 percent of the time, no one questioned them if they behaved confidently and acted like they were *supposed to be there*. More recently, security consultant and social engineer Chris Hadnagy has reported that when people "tailgate" into secure areas by acting like they belong and walking in with confidence they are *successful over 90 percent of the time* in getting past security, because people are hesitant to confront someone who appears to know what they're doing. The bottom line is that people are wired to assume someone belongs if they seem like they do! So walking into a room with confidence, whether it's a gala or a dinner party, automatically announces, "I belong." It's time for *you* to believe this.

On your best days, sure, use that extra juice to pump up your NVC to make an awe-inspiring entrance with a sultry walk. Think Beyoncé...smoldering in action, glowing complexion, hair like a perfectly flowing waterfall. A sultry walk manages to be sensually attractive, alluring, and passionately intense all at once. It's a way to create a mood, look, or atmosphere that exudes desire, seduction, and mystery. This walk is all about embracing your own power, with fluid yet controlled movements that express a quiet, magnetic presence. The sway of your hips, the rhythm of your steps, and the way you hold yourself can create a captivating energy that radiates self-assuredness and an irresistible charm. Walk at a slightly slower pace than usual, making each step deliberate while allowing your body to move fluidly. You want to go for smooth, intentional movements rather than hurried strides. If Patrick Dempsey or Errol Pierre were standing on the other side of the room, you'd walk to him slowly...making him wait for you. This is the time to use those hips. Allow your hips to sway gently and naturally as you walk but keep the movement subtle and controlled. Remember, you're not in a Zumba class. The gentleness is what adds the sense of rhythm and sensuality to your steps, turning heads in the process. But now we've got to get real.

What about an average Tuesday when your day has been booked with back-to-back meetings, your clients needed constant hand-holding, your boss was in a *mood*, and you still want to make an impression at the cocktail party you are attending after work? Let's face it, life isn't cut out for us to look like superstars on a regular basis. I don't have a team of makeup artists and hairstylists on retainer, do you? But this doesn't mean we all can't exude our own personal version of queen power.

Before you enter the event, take a moment to check in with yourself, noticing any negativity that's impacting you mentally or physically—whether you're still thinking about your annoying colleague, or you feel bloated from eating pizza for lunch. Shake that off and be present. A mini ritual can help. Reapply your lipstick, repeat a mantra, or take a quick selfie, look at it, and say, "Whoa, I do look good." Take a breath and now you're good to go.

When you walk into a room, your first impression starts before you say a word, so lead with presence. Stand tall, shoulders back, and move with purpose, as if you belong there (even if you don't feel like it yet). Make eye contact as if every person in the room is there to see you, and you're giving them each a personal greeting with your eyes. Offer up a natural, confident smile—it's a powerful signal that you're open, grounded, and approachable. Do whatever you can to quickly shed your coat and purse; excess baggage, literal or visual, distracts from your presence and can make you appear weighed down or unsure. Strong posture is essential here; the slump ain't ever sexy. Hold your head high, shoulders back, and spine straight. This confident stance instantly commands attention and sets the foundation for your walk. Walk at a slightly slower than normal pace; you're not rushing to cross the street before the light changes. When you stop or reach your destination, pause gracefully. Stand tall, offering a small smile or glance that reinforces your composed, powerful presence. But don't let it go on too long—just enough dazzle to make a lasting impression. You've entered with ease and your body language has made a statement before you've said a word: "I'm here, and I'm meant to be." Again, we are not always trying to pull off a dramatic entrance à la Beyoncé or J.Lo.

A great example is Tracee Ellis Ross, whose posture and presence exude ease and playfulness. Her confidence comes from owning her individuality. She's expressive without being over-the-top and commands attention through her positive vibe, not pop-star glam. Tracee Ellis Ross has a feminine energy that's powerful and inviting, *but real.*

Can we discuss posture specifically for a moment? It's important. You are grown, and long gone are the days of your mother tellin' you to sit up or stand up straight. But it's so important that you do! Bad posture can instantly undermine even the best-dressed, most well-intentioned entrance. Slouched shoulders, a lowered head, or a shuffling gait signal insecurity, disinterest, or lack of self-awareness…none of which inspire confidence or connection. Instead of commanding attention, poor posture repels it, creating an invisible barrier between you and the room. People may not consciously register what's wrong, but they'll feel something's off. A collapsed stance makes you seem smaller, uncertain, or even apologetic for being there, which is exactly the opposite of the energy you want to project. In fact, a 2015 study published in *Health Psychology* found that people who adopted upright posture reported higher self-esteem, improved mood, and less stress—even in pressure-filled situations, proving that posture doesn't just influence how others see you, but how you feel walking in.

Let me turn specifically to my men. Entering a room with presence is just as vital, but the masculine version plays by different rules. A man's presence isn't about grace or charm; it's about power, control, and certainty. When you walk into a room, you're not gliding in—you're claiming territory. Purposeful strides, a grounded stance, shoulders squared and chest open—you move like someone who handles business and doesn't need to explain himself. Eye contact is direct but not aggressive; you're scanning the room like you're assessing it, not asking for approval.

Masculine presence is stillness under pressure—no fidgeting, no pacing, no fixing your tie for the fifth time. And when you speak, your voice doesn't rise to be heard; it stays low and calm, drawing people in with authority, not volume. You're not here to impress; you're here to lead.

Look at Lenny Kravitz. The rocker is the definition of effortless masculine presence. He doesn't enter a room—he glides into it with cool, collected certainty. His energy is unshakable: calm, rooted, and magnetic. He doesn't rush, doesn't posture; he simply arrives, fully himself, and that's enough. Whether he's in a perfectly tailored suit or shirtless with a scarf the size of a blanket, he owns every inch of his space without ever demanding it. His eye contact is steady, his voice smooth and grounded, and his stillness carries more weight than someone twice as loud.

Every event or gathering has a rhythm. Pay attention to the overall vibe and **ADAPT** to the energy of the room. Observe for a moment and calibrate yourself. Is the business meeting animated and fast-paced like a party, or is it more of a subdued, intimate, and relaxed kind of gathering? Adjust your energy accordingly. If the room is lively and high energy, sit at the table tall and double-check that your heart power zone is open. Let your hand gestures be expressive and maintain eye contact with warmth and confidence. Move with purpose, speak with enthusiasm, and engage with dynamic facial expressions. If the room is calm and intimate (like a small gathering or formal setting), adopt a more relaxed stance, soften your gestures, and use slower, more intentional movements. Keep your voice steady and your expressions subtle, signaling attentiveness rather than dominance.

This is where my poor buddy Derek from the previous chapter went really wrong. He did not adapt his energy to the appropriate level. His enthusiasm and excitement would have been more appropriate at a music festival than a job interview. Knowing how to read the room and adapt accordingly with your body, gestures, posture, and tone of voice puts you several steps ahead of the game. The goal is to blend in *before* standing out. When your energy matches the flow of the space, it's like an automatic entrance ticket. It's easy for people to accept you—making it easier for you to engage and make an impact.

Where you **SITUATE** yourself matters; it signals whether or not you are part of the action (we'll dive deeper into the power of positioning later). The good news is that you can position yourself in a high-traffic, low-pressure area, where conversations naturally start. There are usually a few ideal spots at any social gathering. At a party, standing by the food or the bar is the easiest. It's a place that draws everyone, creating easy opportunities for casual small talk. Break the ice with simple comments like "Have you tried this yet?" or "That drink looks interesting! What's it called?" without the pressure of forcing a deep conversation. It's not uncommon for gatherings to have some sort of unique element such as a photo booth, a game, or a station with a signature cocktail—plant yourself nearby.

Let's say you're meeting new team members, and your company has brought in a catered lunch. A simple comment in the buffet line—"Wow, that looks good. By the way, I'm Sally. Welcome to the team! We are excited to have you."—does the job. If just thinking about this makes you anxious, please get ahold of yourself. You are not in your seventh-grade cafeteria on the first day of school. You are not going to be turned away from the popular table! A big part of the EASE method is doing more with less effort. **SITUATE** yourself where social interactions happen organically; this will immediately make you feel like part of the group. It puts you in the flow, making it easier to ease into conversations naturally.

And finally, you're ready to **ENGAGE** with others. I've made it clear that nodding and laughing from the zone of safety doesn't count as real participation. You aren't a bystander in your own life and that means you must contribute! These ideas work in literally any situation where you're expected to socialize, whether it's a party or a work event. Start with basic, low-risk engagement: React to something someone says, ask a question, or introduce yourself. Even small comments like "That's hilarious; what happened next?" or "I love that idea!" show that you're involved and keep a conversation moving forward. *You're grown.* It's time to stop waiting for an invitation and insert yourself into the conversation in a way that feels authentic to you.

I know this can feel like an impossible mission, but we're going to keep it simple: They talk; you talk. Let the other person share something—whether it's a response to a question, an opinion, or a story, and then build on it by adding your own thoughts, experience, or a related question. It's a natural rhythm: listen, respond, share. No need to make it more complicated than that. Stay engaged and let the exchange flow organically rather than overthinking what to say next and falling into an awkward silence.

If you're thinking you'd rather pluck out all the hair in your eyebrows than engage, remember three simple words—observation, compliment, and question—and you'll never feel that stomach-churning anxiety about socializing again. Instead of diving straight into small talk, make an observation about the setting, follow it with a compliment, and then ask a question. It works like this: "This conference has such a positive vibe. I bet you've been here before; you seem like you know the ropes. Any suggestions about which breakout sessions to attend?"

Knowing when to pause can actually help make a person a better conversationalist. People often rush to fill silence, which can be even more awkward than the lull in conversation. A well-timed pause can make your words feel more impactful and draw people in. When someone shares something interesting, instead of immediately responding, pause for a second, nod, and then say something thoughtful, like "That's really interesting. What made you get into that?"

There's another easy technique called "the Flip" that keeps conversations from being basic. Instead of asking something typical, like "What do you do?," be playful and flip the question. For instance, go with something unexpected, like "If you could have any job for a week, just to try it, what would it be?" Or instead of "Where are you from?" try, "If you could live anywhere for a month, where would it be?" Playful questions are fresher and more memorable, and they help break people out of autopilot responses.

Using EASE helps you avoid the social quicksand of lurking and being overlooked. It transforms you from a flat and passive observer to an active participant, making it easier to form real connections instead of just blending into the background. With some practice, you'll never again be drawn to the dark side where the nonsocializers gather. You'll quickly grow confident in your ability to strike up a chat with anyone.

I cannot begin to count the number of people I have worked with who struggle with being flat. I have seen how much anxiety and distress flatness can cause. I want you to take a breath, sit up a little taller, and really let this moment land. Because everything we've talked about...from the awkward silences to the group huddles in the corner to the hovering just outside the circle—all of it comes back to one powerful truth: You were never meant to live flat.

Flatness isn't just a social misstep. It's a symptom of deeper fear: fear of being seen, of being rejected, of not knowing what to say, or of saying the wrong thing. It's the energy of hiding in plain sight. And let me tell you something—flat may feel safe, but it is a lonely place to live. When you choose to stay in the background, to let others do the talking, laughing, and living, you're not avoiding risk; you're avoiding life. That dull, neutral, no-fizz energy isn't protecting you. It's robbing you.

And baby, I see you. I see how much you have to offer. I see the brilliance that's been buried beneath the weight of hesitation and social anxiety. I see the version of you that walks into a room and is fully present. Someone who knows their worth. Who doesn't just take up space but owns it. Who doesn't cling to the sidelines but steps boldly into the dance—whatever that looks like for you. I want you to stop waiting to be chosen, noticed, or validated. I want you to start showing up as if you already belong, because you do. Flatness was never your natural state. You were born vibrant, expressive, dynamic. You just forgot. Or maybe someone told you otherwise, and you believed them. Maybe the world dimmed your light a little, and you adjusted.

But let me be clear: Your light is still there. It's time to turn the brightness all the way up. There will always be a reason to hold back. A reason to stay safe. But that's not the life you want to live. Your presence is your power. It doesn't have to be loud or theatrical. It just has to be real. Honest. You. And when you show up with that kind of truth, people feel it. They respond. You become magnetic—not because you're performing, but because you're connected. Aligned. Alive.

So the next time you're tempted to default to the shadows? I want you to remember this: Flat is forgettable. But you? You were made to shine. No more shovin' yourself into an imaginary lifeboat. No more skulking. From now on, you are the one who walks in, stands tall, meets eyes, and lets your energy speak before your mouth ever opens. From now on, you are a presence in every room you enter…not just a body in the background. Say goodbye to flat and step into the fizz and flavor—let everyone see the essence of who you really are.

***Let me ask you this: Have you ever shaken hands with a limp, wet rag?***

*A handshake with a wet rag is limp, lifeless, and is like grasping onto something that should have structure but doesn't. No grip, no intention, just a soggy afterthought of human contact. It offers no energy, no confidence, just a weak press of fingers that quickly slips away, making the whole exchange feel, well, creepy and gross. It sends the message that you'd rather be anywhere else, or worse, that you have no confidence at all.*

*A proper handshake, on the other hand, is a small but mighty act. You meet the other person's hand with equal pressure—firm, not crushing. A brief, solid grip that conveys confidence and warmth. Your hand should meet the other person's fully and hold it for two to three seconds with a natural shake. Make eye contact, offer a slight smile, and then go for a clean release. A good handshake sets the tone, signaling that you're present, capable, and engaged. That's it. Simple, direct, and memorable. It says you're someone worth taking seriously.*

*While a handshake is widely seen as a standard gesture of greeting or respect in many Western cultures, there are times and places where it can be culturally inappropriate. In some conservative religious communities, particularly within Islamic and Orthodox Jewish traditions, physical contact between men and women who are not related is discouraged or forbidden, meaning a handshake could be seen as disrespectful rather than polite. In parts of Asia, such as Japan or Thailand, bowing is the preferred form of greeting, and a handshake may come across as overly forward or intrusive, especially if it's too firm.*

*Even within cultures where handshakes are common, the context matters...offering your hand too quickly or aggressively, or during moments of grief or solemnity, can feel awkward or insensitive. Being aware of local customs and reading the room before reaching out can show more respect than the gesture itself.*

## Part II
# THE SECRETS

People ask me about my secrets all the time. They really do think I'm some kind of clairvoyant! And while I'll admit it *does* look like magic when you can walk into a room and instantly read the energy, the truth is, it's not about being psychic; it's practice. Nonverbal communication is a hidden language, and once you know what to look for, it's like having X-ray vision in meetings, dates, interviews—any situation where reading the room gives you the edge. The tilt of someone's head, the stillness of their hands, the timing of a glance—all of it speaks in a language you're learning to "speak," giving you valuable information no one else has access to. And the real trick? When you also have control of your own signals, you don't just read the room; you steer it.

The secrets you're about to learn will give you a level of power most people don't even know exists. The following secrets of NVC are all within your grasp, and once you master them, everything gets easier. Whether you want to captivate a room, influence a meeting, or have a strong presence, it all starts with understanding and controlling your body language. When you learn to wield these secrets with precision, you're no longer just reacting to the world—you're shaping it to work in your favor.

## CHAPTER FIVE

# CIA Energy

CIA energy is that next-level awareness, the kind that's so keen it sees beneath the surface of everything. It's the ability to walk into a room and instantly clock the dynamics, sense what people are thinking before they even say a word, and stay three steps ahead without breaking a sweat. It's not about being loud and dramatic—it's the quiet confidence of someone who reads the room like their own personal map. At the core of this secret language are a few crucial building blocks: baselines, clusters, and microexpressions. When you know what's "normal" for someone (their baseline), spot patterns that appear together (clusters), and catch the quick flashes of truth that leak through the face (microexpressions), you don't just see what's happening; you understand *why*. And that understanding not only gives you access to valuable information, but "the knowing" gives you an undeniable allure, an air of mystery, and a level of extra intelligence that people can't quite put their finger on, *but they feel it.*

Real spies aren't like James Bond. They're not having car chases in glamorous settings or ordering martinis at the bar with a wink. In truth, the most skilled intelligence operatives are standing in the room just like everyone else, but they're soaking in *everything* around them like a sponge. Nothing goes unnoticed. They're absorbing body language, tone shifts, eye movements, emotional undercurrents; they're noticing who's nervous, who's dominant, and who's pretending to be someone they're not. They gain power not through spectacle, but through observation. Let's get this same power into *your* hands.

The first step to channeling your CIA energy is familiarizing yourself with the "Seven Microexpressions." Microexpressions are brief, involuntary facial expressions that reveal a person's true emotions, often lasting only a fraction of a second. There are seven universally recognized microexpressions, each corresponding to a basic human emotion: **happiness, sadness, anger, fear, surprise, disgust, and contempt**. These expressions are consistent across cultures and are believed to be biologically hardwired into the human brain.

For example, happiness is shown through raised cheeks and crow's-feet around the eyes, while anger appears with a furrowed brow and tight lips. Fear widens the eyes and raises the eyebrows, whereas disgust wrinkles the nose and raises the upper lip. Surprise is marked by raised eyebrows and an open mouth, sadness features drooping eyelids and a downturned mouth, and contempt is uniquely shown with a one-sided mouth raise. These expressions happen so quickly that they're easy to miss, but mastering the ability to read them can provide deep insight into what someone is truly feeling, regardless of what they say. But girl, these expressions will vanish faster than a Taylor Swift concert sells out, so get to work to recognize these info-packed gems.

How many of you parents of tweens and teens can relate to this scenario: Imagine that your daughter walks in the door and you turn from the stove and glance at her—you see the slight slump of her shoulders and the way her hoodie's sleeves are pulled down over her hands. She sits at the kitchen table while you wait for the kettle to boil. It's automatic, you ask how school was, and she gives her usual response: "Fine." But today, something is off. Your daughter looks up at you to accept a mug of tea, and that's when you see it. A quick flicker, gone in an instant. Your daughter's eyes darted away too fast. The corners of her mouth twitched downward for less than a second before settling into a neutral line. There was tension in her jaw that hadn't been there yesterday. You let a few quiet moments pass before gently saying, "You don't have to talk about it if you're not ready. But I can see something's bothering you."

She doesn't move at first, but then she blinks. Her lower lip trembles for a moment before she presses it shut. Her hands curl tighter around the mug. "It's Zoe," she says finally, her voice barely above a whisper as she talks about her best friend. "I think she's not eating. Like…really not eating." You feel her concern in your heart. "What makes you think that?" "She skips lunch. Says she's full when we hang out. She's lost a lot of weight. But it's not just that. She gets angry if I ask about it. And today she said she was just tired, but I saw her knees shaking." Your girl's eyes well up with tears. "I didn't know if I should tell anyone. I don't want her to hate me." You reach across the table and cover her hands with your own. "You did the right thing by saying something. Let's figure out the next step together. You're not alone in this." By observing such a small shift in your daughter, a serious situation is brought to light and the appropriate action can be taken to get her friend some help.

Since microexpressions cover nearly the entire span of human emotions (these expressions were identified by the psychologist Paul Ekman, whom you're going to learn more about soon), the information they relay can help maximize your responses to get the best outcome in both positive and negative situations (like with Zoe).

Jared was interviewing for a position he really wanted, one that felt just slightly out of reach. Halfway through the interview, the CEO asked, "How would you handle a team member who keeps missing deadlines?" Jared gave his well-rehearsed response, something about proactive communication and accountability. But as he finished, he caught a flash on her face: a brief narrowing of the eyes and a tightening around her mouth. It was subtle, but to Jared, it registered as doubt.

Maybe his answer had sounded too textbook, so he pivoted, adding, "Actually...if I'm being totally honest, I've worked with someone like that before. At first, I tried structure and reminders, but what really made the difference was realizing they were totally overwhelmed and too afraid to ask for help. Once I opened that door, we got back on track. It taught me not to assume what the problem is without really listening first."

That's when he saw it. The CEO's eyes softened, and her mouth pulled into the beginning of a real smile. Three days later, he got the job offer. Understanding microexpressions was the icing on the cake that got Jared his dream job, and they also kept Nina from losing hers. Nina had been at the company four years, long enough to recognize when something was off. Projects had been slowing down, and leadership had gone oddly quiet in the last few weeks. So, during a team meeting, she raised her hand and asked, trying to keep her voice even, "Are there any plans for layoffs?"

Her manager smiled quickly—too quickly. "No, absolutely not. Everything's stable. We're just refocusing a few priorities." But Nina caught it. Before the smile, before the polished answer, there was a split-second shift in his face: His lips pressed together tightly, his chin dropped ever so slightly, and his eyebrows rose in a flash of worry. It was gone as fast as it came, replaced with calm corporate-speak. But it was enough. He was hiding something. Nina didn't challenge him, but that night she updated her résumé and reached out to a few people in her network. Within a week, she had two informational interviews lined up. A month later and just days before the layoffs were formally announced, she accepted a new and bigger role at a smaller but growing company.

Microexpressions are more than fleeting facial tics; they're powerful signals that, when read accurately, offer both protection and an advantage. As a form of emotional X-ray, they reveal truth beneath the surface, allowing you to spot deception, defuse tension, or recognize danger before it escalates.

But beyond safety, they're also a sharp tool of influence. When you can detect even a flicker of hesitation, discomfort, or interest, you gain the upper hand—adjusting your words, tone, or timing to shift outcomes in your favor. In essence, microexpressions are both armor and strategy: They keep you safe and make you more effective.

Once you've gotten to know the seven microexpressions, you'll be in the unique position to identify "leakage." No, I'm not talking about faulty taps—I'm talking about emotional leakage. Paul Ekman, the renowned American psychologist best known for his groundbreaking work in the study of facial expressions, emotions, and nonverbal communication, defines "leakage" as "the involuntary emotional expressions that occur despite a person's attempt to conceal or mask their true feelings."

In his research on deception and facial expressions, leakage refers specifically to the brief, often subconscious displays of genuine emotion, typically through microexpressions, voice tone, posture, or gestures that "leak out" even when someone is trying to suppress or fake a *different emotion*. Ekman discovered that leakage is strongest in the face (especially the micro-muscles around the eyes and mouth), the voice, and body movements, and it often occurs during high-stakes situations when someone is under pressure to lie or withhold their true emotional state.

Let's look at some scenarios in day-to-day life where leakage could easily occur, when a person's true emotions momentarily slip through, revealing the exact feelings they're trying to conceal. For example, during a job interview a candidate might be asked if they feel confident handling high-pressure situations. They respond with a calm, "Yes, absolutely. I thrive under pressure." However, just before they speak, their eyebrows rise and draw together, their eyes widen (classic signs of fear), and their hand goes to the suprasternal notch (the visible dip or hollow at the base of the throat) located between the two clavicles (collarbones) at the top of the sternum (breastbone), a common form of self-soothing. Despite their confident words, their face leaks anxiety, suggesting they may not feel as secure as they claim.

In another instance, someone at a dinner party is handed a homemade dish and politely says, "Mmm, thank you! This looks delicious." But wait for it! For a split second, their upper lip lifts and their nose wrinkles, revealing a flash of disgust. Though they quickly recover with a smile, that involuntary expression betrays their true reaction to the food. These brief flashes, often lasting less than a quarter of a second, are powerful indicators of hidden emotion, and being able to spot them can offer deep insight into what someone is really feeling beneath the surface.

Understanding leakage is like having a crystal ball for human emotion—it offers a glimpse into what someone is truly feeling, even when they're trying to hide it. These lightning-fast blasts of authenticity—an eye twitch, a lip curl, or a flicker of fear—reveal more than words ever could. When you can spot leakage, you're not just reading people; you're reading *through* them. It's like seeing the truth before it's spoken, giving you the power to anticipate reactions, uncover hidden agendas, or connect on a deeper level. In high-stakes situations, it's not just insight—it's an edge.

Training yourself to notice and identify microexpressions boils down to mindfulness and lots of practice. Learning to read microexpressions starts with training your eye for speed and subtlety. These expressions often flash across the face in less than half a second, so it's essential to practice recognizing them in real time. One effective tip is to study those seven universal emotions (happiness, sadness, anger, fear, surprise, disgust, and contempt) using slowed-down videos to see what each expression looks like at its peak. Second, train with real-world observation: Watch interviews, reality shows, or debates with the sound off, and try to guess what someone is feeling based purely on facial cues. Third, regularly observe people's reactions in various settings. You might be jogging on the treadmill at the gym, but your real purpose is to practice noticing microexpressions. The flashes are everywhere. You may notice a flash of contempt as a trainer coaches a client who isn't following his advice. Finally, pay close attention to mismatches between expressions and words. If someone says, "I'm fine," with a quick flash of sadness or contempt like our worried teen, that leak may tell you the real story. The more you practice, the more your brain starts catching what others miss, and I promise you the work is worth it.

Understanding NVC gives you an extra edge, allowing you to see beyond words and decode what people are truly thinking and feeling. But to truly tap into CIA energy, you must utilize "baselines" and "clusters," which are both essential if you want to make accurate readings of someone's behavior. Reading into a single gesture can lead to false conclusions, which only cause problems and don't help you with a darn thing. Let's be honest, have you ever written someone off because of a single negative interaction? Or maybe someone caught you in a bad moment and decided you had a terrible personality. Has something like this ever happened to you?

Enjoying iced tea on the front porch, Lisa leaned toward Emily and whispered, "That new neighbor, Claire? She's mean. When I introduced myself, she barely smiled, crossed her arms, and gave these short, clipped answers like she couldn't wait to get away from me." Emily frowned. "Really? That's disappointing. I guess we won't be asking her to join our poker night."

A few days later, they ran into Claire at a neighborhood cookout, and to their surprise, she was completely different. Claire was warm, smiling, chatting easily, and even cracking jokes. It turned out Claire wasn't mean at all; she was just caught in a bad moment. "Oh, I feel terrible about the other day!" Claire said. "I meant to come over and apologize. I had just gotten off a stressful call when you stopped by. I wasn't trying to be rude. My grandmother is in the hospital." Emily and Lisa exchanged a glance, realizing they had misjudged her. Good thing they realized it too—Claire turned out to be a helluva poker player and she always brought the best snacks. Misunderstandings like this are common, and to be able to read someone's NVC accurately, you need to start by finding a baseline and identifying clusters of cues before you go and get all judgy.

A baseline refers to a person's normal, relaxed behavior—their natural way of expressing themselves when they're not under stress or attempting to deceive. It includes their typical facial expressions, tone of voice, posture, gestures, and eye movement patterns. Establishing a baseline is essential because deviations from it—such as a sudden shift in body language, a forced smile, or a change in voice pitch—can signal that something is off, such as discomfort, dishonesty, or emotional stress. Without a baseline, it's easy to misread normal behavior as suspicious or unusual, so observing someone in low-pressure situations first helps you detect when something truly changes.

Assuming the new neighbor is mean because she was rushed and closed off during one interaction is not taking into account her baseline behavior. If old Mrs. Jones down the block has always had her arms crossed and a scowl on her face every time you've seen her since you moved in a decade ago, deeming her cranky is, well, fair. Now, let's say Uncle George scratches his beard constantly. You know this is normal behavior for him, but if someone were to make a judgment based on one meeting, their response might be, "What's up with that guy? Is he confused or pondering the meaning of life?" What seems strange isn't necessarily strange if it turns out to be baseline behavior.

The best way to establish someone's baseline behavior is to observe them in neutral situations. You want a stress-free scenario. During a performance review, a first date, or even while watching a football game is not the time to study baselines (nothing revs people up like sports). An ideal option is during a casual conversation or while they are listening to someone speaking so you can notice their regular body language when they are not feeling pressured, nervous, or defensive. Pay attention to their posture, facial expressions, hand gestures, and the eye contact they exhibit.

Over time (that's right; this isn't something you can determine in five minutes), you'll notice certain patterns in the way someone behaves. Do they typically sit with arms crossed, or are they usually more open? Do they often smile or maintain a neutral expression when they chat? Some people may have habitual gestures, like playing with their hair (or their beard like Uncle George), tapping their foot, or using their hands when they talk. These habitual gestures are part of their baseline, so when you see these behaviors later, you won't misinterpret them as signs of nervousness or deceit. These unique and consistent physical behaviors add up to a person's baseline.

When someone deviates from their baseline, it means their behavior has shifted from what's normal or typical for them, and that change often signals something significant. For example, if a person who usually speaks with steady eye contact suddenly avoids your gaze, or someone who's typically relaxed starts fidgeting or stammering, those deviations could indicate discomfort, stress, deception, or emotional conflict—there's something going on. The key isn't in the behavior itself, but in the change from their norm. By first observing a person's baseline, you can spot these subtle shifts more accurately and interpret them as potential clues to what's really going on beneath the surface.

Clusters refer to groups of body language signals that appear together and reinforce the same message or emotional state. A single gesture—like crossing arms or scratching the nose—can be ambiguous on its own, but when it appears alongside other consistent cues (like a tight jaw, averted eyes, and a closed posture), it forms a cluster that strengthens the interpretation, such as defensiveness or discomfort. Reading clusters helps avoid misjudging isolated actions and provides a more accurate, reliable picture of what a person is truly feeling or communicating. The more signals that align, the clearer the message becomes.

When you spot a cluster of nonverbal cues, you want to interpret the message behind it, not react to a single gesture and then decide what to do based on the context. Clusters help you decode someone's emotional state more accurately, whether it's discomfort, confidence, dishonesty, openness, or something else. Once you understand the emotional undercurrent, you can adjust your own behavior or approach accordingly.

For example, if you're in a negotiation and you notice a cluster of cues coming from the person on the other side of the table—tight lips, arms crossed, feet pointed toward the door—you might recognize resistance or hesitation. Instead of pushing harder, you could slow down, ask clarifying questions, or offer reassurance to rebuild comfort.

In a conversation at work, if someone's verbal message is "I'm fine" but their body language cluster screams sadness or tension, you might choose to gently follow up or give them space, depending on the situation. The goal isn't to confront or call it out; it's to respond with greater emotional intelligence. Clusters give you insight; what you decide to do next determines your effectiveness.

Being able to accurately identify clusters and baselines gives you a powerful advantage in both your personal and professional life. It's like unlocking a hidden layer of conversation that most people miss. When you can read someone's baseline behavior and spot meaningful deviations, you're better equipped to sense when someone is uncomfortable, withholding information, facing a personal struggle, or not fully aligned with their words. Recognizing clusters of body language lets you interpret emotions with far more accuracy, helping you navigate sensitive situations, build trust more quickly, and make smarter decisions. Whether you're negotiating a deal, comforting a friend, leading a team, or simply trying to connect more deeply with others, this skill makes you more perceptive, responsive, and influential, giving you an edge that feels almost intuitive.

If you play poker, you're probably aware of the concept of "tells," but there is much to be learned from them beyond the card game. If you watch closely, people will eventually "surrender their tells." Tells are subtle, often unconscious behaviors that reveal a person's true thoughts, emotions, or intentions, especially when they're trying to conceal them. These cues can show up in facial expressions, body language, tone of voice, gestures, or even repeated habits, and they tend to leak out during moments of stress, excitement, or deception. Unlike microexpressions, which are universal and rooted in biology, tells are often unique to the individual and must be learned through careful observation over time. For example, one person might always scratch their neck when they're unsure, while another might fidget with a ring when they're hiding something.

Let's start with that classic setting where tells become crucial: the poker table. Imagine a high-stakes game where players are trying to bluff their way to a win. One player might glance at their chips more often when they have a strong hand, or another might suddenly stop talking when they're bluffing. Even a subtle shift, like holding their breath or tapping their foot, can give them away. Experienced players study their opponents, not just for what they do, but for how their behavior changes under pressure. In this way, tells become silent giveaways, and the ability to read them can mean the difference between folding too soon or calling a bluff and walking away with the pot.

Even the best poker players can drop a tell under pressure. One of the most famous tells in poker history came from the legendary player Johnny Chan. In the 1988 World Series of Poker Main Event, Chan's heads-up match against Erik Seidel was so iconic, it was later dramatized in the movie *Rounders* in 1998 starring Matt Damon. In the final round, Erik Seidel is holding a decent hand and trying to decide whether to call Johnny Chan's big bet. Seidel sits silently, staring at his chips, and then he freezes. He stops moving completely, a classic "freeze response" that can happen under psychological pressure. His stillness was likely an unconscious attempt to not give anything away, but for seasoned players like Chan, this was itself a tell.

Johnny Chan, calm and composed, sat back, twirled his orange chip, and stared across the table. He read Seidel's frozen posture not as strength, but as hesitation and discomfort, a sign of a player who wasn't confident in his hand. Chan trusted the read and pressed the bet. Seidel called and Chan won the championship. The tell wasn't a twitch or a glance; it was the absence of normal behavior, a subtle freeze, which Chan recognized as a sign of vulnerability. That ability to read emotional states through nonverbal cues gave him a psychological edge, proof that even in the quietest moments, our bodies speak.

While I hope the information I'm sharing improves your poker game, let's look at how being able to identify tells helps you out in the world. Reading tells, the subtle often unconscious signals people give off, can reveal what words don't say, and this skill is invaluable both in life and at work. Take Maya, for instance. Her friends are celebrating her recent breakup with Kevin, a guy they simply could not stand, and they're thrilled she's on the dating scene again. But when someone casually mentions, "I'm so glad you dumped Kevin; I heard he's with some new girl now. Can't imagine what she sees in him," Maya's smile falters for just a second. Her eyes drop and her jaw tightens, betraying a pang of lingering attachment. That flicker says more than a monologue could: She's not fully over him. Get out the cheesecake because your girlfriend still needs some support!

At work, the same skill can give you a secret advantage. Imagine you're pitching a new idea in a meeting, and your boss is nodding along, giving polite affirmations. You've seen over time how when she doesn't like something her foot begins tapping faster, her lips press tightly together, and there's a slight narrowing of the eyes. She's not convinced, even if she just won't say it outright. Catching that in real time lets you adjust course, ask a question, clarify a point, or change your tone so you can pivot before the opportunity slips away. Tells give you precious insight beneath the surface, helping you respond to what people *really* feel, not just what they say.

Everything we've discussed in this chapter, such as learning to read baselines and microexpressions, detecting leakage, and finding clusters and tells, is like unlocking a secret language, a language most people don't even realize they're speaking. With every glance, gesture, and flicker of emotion, you're tuning in to a deeper layer of truth. And as this new fluency grows, so does something else: a kind of quiet, magnetic confidence. The more you see, the less you have to guess. That's the CIA energy I'm talking about. It's not loud or showy—you don't need to drive an Aston Martin or wear a tuxedo. It's precise. It's the subtle sense that you know something others don't, that you see what's unspoken. People feel it. They lean in, they trust, they wonder. You start to carry yourself differently—not because you have all the answers, but because you know how to read the room long before most people even know there is something to read. It's not just about winning. It's about becoming the kind of person who always seems to know exactly what to do, and that kind of knowing brings its own style of power. Now go ahead and get yourself a martini because you sure earned it. Shaken not stirred, of course.

***Let me ask you this:***
***Do you know what your own tells are?***

*Learning to recognize your own tells is like holding up a mirror to your subconscious; it gives you powerful insight into how others may be reading you, even when you think you're keeping it cool. Start by noticing how your body reacts in moments of stress, excitement, or discomfort. Do you touch your face when you're nervous? Cross your arms when you feel defensive? Glance away when you're unsure? One of the best ways to uncover your own tells is to watch yourself in action. Record a mock conversation, presentation, or even a casual video chat. Then review it like you're watching someone else: Where does your energy leak? What gestures don't match your words? You can also ask a trusted friend to give feedback on your nonverbal habits. The goal isn't to become robotic or hypercontrolled; it's to become self-aware enough that you can align your body language with your true intentions or at least know when you're giving more away than you meant to.*

## CHAPTER SIX

# How to Spot a Deceiver

Love can make us blind, but I'm going to open your eyes. One of my girlfriends called me not too long ago and said, "Linda, I met this amazing man. I just know he's 'the One.' I need you to come to dinner with us and do your thing...you know, check him out."

"You know my price, right?" I said, laughing. My price is dinner at a very high-end restaurant of my choosing. I meet my girlfriend Gloria on Friday night at a new, highly reviewed restaurant I've wanted to try. We're at the table catching up when a tall, good-looking man saunters in. I clock that he seems hesitant to sit down when he sees me at the table, and I catch an eyebrow flash that could indicate he's surprised to see me. I open up with some basic small talk, mentioning the beautiful weather and how elegant the restaurant is before I say, "So, how long have you been dating?" His name is Carlos, and

I notice he's rubbing his thighs, a sign that he's uncomfortable. Then he answers after a fairly long pause, like he had to think about it: "Oh, about three months?" I can already tell this man is hiding something and he's up to no good, but I'm keeping things light—not going in for the kill quite yet.

I study my menu intensely, like it's a thrilling crime novel, to create a pause before I speak: "Wow, these stuffed mushrooms look fantastic. And the fish sounds good too. What a unique preparation." Then I slowly lean in, with a neutral look on my face, and ask, "Tell me, Carlos, have you ever been married?" My simple question really gets his fight-or-flight instincts going.

When a person feels threatened or overwhelmed, the brain's amygdala kicks into high alert. This tiny, almond-shaped cluster deep in the brain is responsible for detecting danger, and when it senses a threat, real or perceived, it doesn't wait for a logical explanation. It hijacks the nervous system, flooding the body with stress hormones like adrenaline and cortisol. This sets off the classic fight-or-flight response: Muscles tense, the heart races, breathing quickens, and the body prepares either to confront the danger or to run from it. In that moment, rational thinking takes a back seat because survival (in this case, not getting on the wrong side of Gloria) is the brain's top priority.

Now his face is frozen. His hands stop moving on his thighs and he leans way back in his chair to create distance. His reaction is full of information. It is clear as day to me that this man is *not* single. I know he's lyin' to Gloria and I'm not the slightest bit surprised based on the signs I'm seeing. (My suspicions were later confirmed by Gloria: He was married.) We spend the rest of the dinner enjoying the food and keeping the conversation light and polite. Carlos is not engaging much with Gloria, who is still flirting away. There are no smiles across the table; he doesn't send her any warm looks, or even ask her a simple question like "How's your entrée?" He knows he's busted and it's awkward. He eats as fast as he can, like he's getting ready to flee, which he does, after making up an excuse about having to be somewhere and he's running late. Good riddance.

The next day Gloria calls me. "Girl, that went well, right? I see you like Carlos. Ya'll got along well enough; too bad he had to leave early, though." Were we at the same dinner? I swear I can feel her smiling through gritted teeth through the phone. I take a couple of beats of silence before answering her, and that has tipped her off that she's not going to like what I have to say. Once I start going into my analysis, I can hear a brutal combination of anger, disappointment, and heartbreak in her voice. "I'll call you back," she says, in a clipped and sad tone. Ten minutes later I see Gloria's number on my phone. "Well, I don't know how you knew, but you were right. That dog is married!" The man started showing all the traits of a liar the very second he arrived; they were evident to me from the start. I'm sorry for Gloria's latest heartbreak, but now that I've taught Gloria what to look out for, her days of dating married jerks are over. I'm going to teach you these clear-cut signs right now so you can spot a conscious deceiver in dating, work, parenting, or any other area of your life.

One of the most well-known verses in the Ten Commandments is "Thou shalt not bear false witness against thy neighbor." In other words, *no lyin'*. But the reality is, lying is a common aspect of human behavior, encompassing those minor "white lies" as well as more significant acts of deception. For most people, lying is infrequent and often socially motivated, such as telling a little white lie to avoid hurting someone's feelings. Are you really going to tell your five-year-old nephew that the drawing he made for you is terrible?

But here's where it gets interesting. In a 2010 study by Dr. Kim Serota, Dr. Timothy Levine, and Franklin J. Boster surveying a thousand adults in the United States, they found that on average people tell one to two lies per day. But they also discovered that the truth about lying is more complex than it appears. While most people tell very few lies, a small subset of individuals—about 5 percent—are responsible for nearly half of all the lies! In other words, a minority of "prolific liars" account for most of the deception. They are comfortable with lying and do it habitually. These are the people I'm going to teach you to watch out for so they can't work their way into your life and wreak havoc.

These prolific liars, or "Conscious Deceivers," use deception more strategically, often in an elaborate fashion for their own personal gain. Conscious deceivers are able to rationalize their deception, believing they are justified in their actions and that their lies are harmless. We all know they are not. Lies like misleading others on purpose are thankfully less common, but the consequences can cause long-lasting damage.

Amanda C. Riley, the subject of the podcast *Scamanda*, deceived her entire community, friends, church congregation, and kindhearted strangers for years by fabricating a cancer diagnosis, soliciting over $100,000 in donations for nonexistent treatments. Similarly, Belle Gibson, an Australian wellness influencer whose story is told in the documentary *Apple Cider Vinegar* on Netflix, falsely claimed to have cured her terminal brain cancer through natural remedies, amassing significant financial gain before the truth of her deceit was exposed. People tend to hear stories like this and say, "Oh, I would never fall for that!" If you think you are too smart to fall for the lies of a conscious deceiver, think again.

Jenifer Faison probably isn't all that different from most of you reading this book. A successful reality television producer who lived in Los Angeles, her life became a fairy tale when she reconnected with her college sweetheart, Spencer Herron, after two decades apart. Their rekindled romance was so passionate she left her glamorous life in Los Angeles to move to a small town in Georgia to be with him. They got married, bought their dream house, and even opened a wine bar together. Jenifer was madly in love, and Spencer left her sweet notes expressing undying love for her before he left for work *every* morning.

Everything looked idyllic until the police came and literally knocked down the front door of their picture-perfect house. Jenifer's world unraveled when Herron was arrested for sexually assaulting a high school student at the school where he taught…and get this, he was even once awarded "Teacher of the Year"! It didn't take long to discover his extensive string of infidelity with numerous women, including some women in her own circle of friends! Spencer had been living a double life throughout their marriage right under her nose; the man even conducted some of his trysts in the wine bar they owned together after hours!

Smart people fall for conscious deceivers all the time. Intelligence doesn't make any of us immune to emotional manipulation, cognitive biases (we'll take a deeper dive into those later), or social conditioning. Ironically, our confidence in our own intelligence can lead us to believe we are too savvy to fall for this nonsense, making us behave with less caution. Conscious deceivers are expert at using urgency, fear, or excitement to override logical thinking, and the element of romance in Jenifer's example made it even easier.

Learning to recognize conscious deceivers is essential—you never want to let one work their way into your life. Obviously, you don't want your life to turn into a cautionary tale like Jenifer Faison's. You want the people you regularly interact with to value honesty. For example, you don't want Kyle to take all the credit for your hard work on the Big Account when you are gunning for a promotion. Nor do you want a new girlfriend to give you a sob story about how she was mugged, and the thief took off with the designer handbag you let her borrow, only to find she's putting on a show. She's cryin' on your shoulder when the truth is she sold it and kept the cash!

Detecting deception can be challenging, but patterns of dishonesty tend to announce themselves over time, like with my girlfriend's date, Carlos. An isolated lie may be difficult to identify, but *repeated* inconsistencies in body language, speech patterns, and behavior can provide clues. Identifying a liar through body language requires observing multiple cues rather than relying on a single tell. While no gesture or movement alone can confirm a deception, it's those clusters of behaviors that set the alarm off that someone is being less than truthful.

Liars come in all shapes and sizes, but knowing the usual behaviors can help you avoid getting involved in a messy and potentially dangerous situation. One of the most revealing signs is inconsistent facial expressions. This is where knowing your microexpressions is like having a secret weapon. Liars often display microexpressions, those lightning-fast, involuntary displays of true emotions that last less than a second before they disappear. You might see fleeting fear, guilt, or distress before a "mechanical smile" appears.

A mechanical smile often looks strained and unnatural, lacking the warmth and spontaneity of a genuine one. However, the most telling sign is in the eyes. While a real smile causes the eyes to crinkle at the corners and light up, a mechanical one leaves the eyes blank, wide, or disconnected from the rest of the expression. In other words, there are no telltale cues of the Duchenne smile we've talked about. Instead, the mouth may be pulled back horizontally rather than curving upward, creating a stretched or stiff appearance, sometimes bordering on a grimace. This kind of smile typically involves only the lower half of the face, with the cheeks failing to rise naturally. There's often visible tension around the jaw or mouth, and the smile may appear and vanish abruptly, without the lingering softness of an authentic expression. Additionally, mechanical smiles can be slightly lopsided or uneven, unlike the more symmetrical quality of a genuine one. They commonly surface in uncomfortable social situations, during polite small talk, or when someone is trying to hide irritation, stress, or disinterest. Think of what your face might look like when a person keeps talking to you—*going on and on*, even though you've clearly said you're late for an appointment and you've really got to go!

A famous example of this occurred in 1998 when President Bill Clinton denied having an affair with Monica Lewinsky. Many people even remember his specific wording because it was oddly formal (another clue): "I did not have sexual relations with that woman." The entire country was watching; Clinton's situation was not only emotionally charged; the stakes were also incredibly high. That's what led to his NVC betraying him before the words left his mouth. In Clinton's case, his facial expressions briefly revealed signs of his internal conflict: Tension and distress marched quickly across his face before he regained composure. This kind of microexpression can be a key indicator of deception. It suggests, in that split second, his true feelings leaked out before he could mask them. Specifically, the tension may have shown up as a tightening of the jaw, furrowing of the brow, or a flash of fear or anger in the eyes. These expressions contradict the calm confidence typically associated with truth-telling. The fact that he quickly composed himself afterward can also be telling; liars often have to concentrate more to maintain a false story, and that effort can cause visible strain. In the context of denying a sexual relationship with Lewinsky, something he later admitted to, these signs of emotional leakage were subtle red flags. They revealed a disconnect between his words and his emotional state, which can be a key indicator that someone is not being truthful.

If you're thinking that finding deception in the eyes sounds challenging, I can't argue with you. This is difficult at first, especially since many signs of lying in the eyes are subtle and easy to miss. But with a little awareness and a lot of practice, you will start to notice the patterns. Ultimately, this is what you need to look for. First, look for incongruence. Pay attention to whether the eyes match the emotion being expressed. If someone is smiling but their eyes are flat or expressionless, it could be a sign the smile is fake and the emotion being presented isn't genuine.

Next, look for eye contact extremes. Liars often fall into one of two camps: (1) Too little eye contact because they feel anxious or guilty. Think of a small child whose mother has asked if he's taken another cookie. He's not likely to make eye contact with Mom, because he knows he's about to get busted. Or (2) too much eye contact, which is an attempt on the part of the liar to prove they're being honest. Use your gut here too. If what's happening with the eye contact feels unnatural to you—it's too evasive or too intense—you may be in the presence of a conscious deceiver.

You also want to notice other forms of eye movement. Look for microexpressions in the eye area. Before a lie is fully delivered, a splash of guilt, fear, or anxiety can show up in the eyes. This might look like widened eyes, a quick squint, or a sudden narrowing—tiny, fleeting expressions that disappear in less than a second. Blinking patterns also hold information. Under the stress of lying, people tend to blink faster or go through short bursts of excessive blinking. On the flip side, some liars blink less when focused on fabricating a story. It depends on the person, which is why those baseline behaviors we talked about are key. Everyone has unique eye behaviors. The key is to observe someone when they're relaxed and telling the truth so you can spot these deviations when they're under pressure or being deceptive. With lots of practice, you can train yourself to catch these microexpressions and reap the benefits of knowing all the information everyone else is missing. Let me show you what I mean.

When Lance Armstrong publicly denied using performance-enhancing drugs during his cycling career, it was his eyes that betrayed him; the man's eyes exhibited every lyin' signal in the book! One of the most telling aspects was that even when his words were firm and confident there was a lack of emotional congruence in his gaze. While his voice remained steady and his statements were direct, his eyes often appeared flat, guarded, and disconnected. There was a noticeable absence of the warmth, openness, or genuine conviction that typically accompanies truth-telling, especially when defending one's integrity. In moments when he was most adamant about being clean, Armstrong's eye contact became intense, bordering on overcompensating. This kind of sustained, almost defiant stare can sometimes be a strategy to appear more credible, but it can also signal a conscious effort to control perception.

At other points, he would blink rapidly or shift his gaze briefly right before delivering a denial—subtle signs of cognitive strain and emotional tension. These microbehaviors, though fleeting, hinted at the internal conflict between what he was saying and what he knew to be true. It wasn't just one expression or moment that gave him away; it was the pattern. The eyes, which we all know are the windows to the soul, revealed a disconnect between his outer confidence and his inner truth. When Armstrong finally confessed, these earlier signs gained new clarity: They weren't just nerves or intensity; they were emotional leakage, the unspoken truth slipping out through his gaze.

Sudden mood swings, such as moving from calm to defensive or aggressive when being questioned, can also point toward someone hiding the truth. Lance Armstrong also did this when he displayed sudden shifts in mood, from calm or joking to aggressive or defensive during media interviews. In 2005, in an interview with Larry King, Armstrong laughed off allegations, calling them "ridiculous" or "witch hunts," but when pressed further, he would shift to a more combative tone, sometimes questioning the credibility of journalists or accusers.

Liars often display their deception in body movements too. Jussie Smollett's 2019 case became a high-profile example of deceptive behavior under public scrutiny. When Smollett gave his first televised interview following his claim of being the victim of a hate crime, he spoke with emotion and conviction, but his body told a more complicated story. Throughout the interview, Smollett frequently touched his face, especially around the mouth and nose. These are common self-soothing gestures that can signal stress or discomfort. His posture often appeared slightly collapsed, with his shoulders pulled inward, suggesting a subconscious attempt to shield himself.

He also exhibited asymmetrical facial expressions, such as one-sided eyebrow lifts or uneven smiles when discussing this serious experience, which can indicate conflicting internal states or a lack of genuine emotion. There were moments when he described the alleged attack that his gestures sometimes didn't align with the gravity of his words. His facial expressions appeared "overcontrolled," meaning they looked too carefully managed or stiff. It was as if he was trying to look a certain way rather than naturally feeling it. Overcontrolled facial expressions often lack the spontaneity, fluidity, or subtle muscle movements that come with genuine emotion.

Smollett's body was also unusually still, except for moments where he seemed to release tension by licking his lips or clearing his throat, which are classic signs of internal anxiety or cognitive strain. After investigations revealed that the attack was staged, Smollett's earlier body language became a focal point in analyzing how deception can leak through even the most emotionally convincing performance. His case is a perfect example of how liars may simultaneously overact and overcontrol, creating a mismatch between the body and the story. When people tell the truth, their gestures naturally align with their speech.

Another telltale sign of liars is that they tend to "pause and hesitate" more often as they construct their responses. They may also alter their speech rate and tone, speaking too quickly or too slowly, or their pitch may rise due to their nervousness.

The use of excessive filler words, such as "um" and "uh," can signal discomfort *but also* the need for extra thinking time.

O. J. Simpson, during his 1994 police interrogation, often hesitated before answering direct questions and sometimes provided vague, noncommittal responses. On June 13, 1994, during a police interview the day after the murders of Nicole Brown Simpson and Ron Goldman, two detectives interviewed Simpson at his home in Brentwood, California. The detectives noticed a cut on his left hand and asked how it happened. Simpson gave a confusing and shifting explanation, hesitating frequently while he struggled to offer a clear timeline. Here's a paraphrased example from the transcript that shows his hesitation and use of filler words when responding to a straightforward question:

**Detective:** "How did you get the cut on your hand?"
**Simpson:** (Pauses) "I…I don't know. I, uh…I cut it on…I don't know, maybe when I broke the glass. I…I had a glass in my hand and, you know, it broke."
**Detective:** "When did this happen?"
**Simpson:** "Last night. Well, I don't know…I think I did it last night. I was rushing around."

He initially says he doesn't know, then gives a vague answer about breaking a glass, followed by more uncertain phrasing about when exactly it occurred. Later in the interview, his explanation shifts slightly, referencing different timelines and scenarios, including cutting himself on a cell phone or during a fit of frustration. This type of noncommittal but also hesitant response, especially when answering a direct question, is a classic example of evasiveness under pressure.

While our focus has been on nonverbal communication, I would be remiss if I didn't share some important phrasing you should be aware of when it comes to liars. For example, some conscious deceivers are able to steer clear of phrases like "I don't remember" or "I guess so," while still avoiding specifics. Elizabeth Holmes, in interviews about Theranos, the health technology company she founded in 2003 that claimed to have developed a revolutionary device that could run hundreds of medical tests using just a few drops of blood from a finger prick, gave responses that were optimistic and filled with visionary language, while avoiding the truth about her failing technology. Some of her responses included: "We are on the brink of completely transforming healthcare as we know it"; "We're seeing extremely promising results in our validation studies"; "Unfortunately, we can't share specifics because our technology is proprietary"; and "We've built a world-class team of scientists and engineers, including people from Apple, Genentech, and the military." Holmes avoided direct answers about progress by elevating the conversation to their future-focused mission. She'd mention data but did not give any specifics, making it sound as if things were going well. Secrecy was her go-to answer for any questions about her technology, and finally she'd name-drop to the moon and back to boost her credibility, making what she was working on seem like an actual possibility when the truth was her company was on the verge of collapse.

Vague answers are a red flag because they point toward a liar who is trying to protect themselves. The less detail they give, the less there is to check, contradict, or catch them in. Sharing specifics can lock a person into a version of events, while being vague provides an opportunity to adapt or shift the story later. This is also a way for a liar to minimize risk—solid details can expose motive, timeline, or inconsistencies. Without them, it's harder for someone to poke holes in the story. Overall, when it comes to deception detection, people who are telling the truth are generally more comfortable being specific because they're recalling or talking about real events. Liars tend to stick to generalities to avoid getting tripped up.

I want to arm you with this information, but I also want my brothers and sisters who have been lied to or cheated on to know that *you are not alone*. Whether it was a boyfriend like Carlos with secrets in his back pocket, a friend who spun a story for sympathy, or someone who smiled at you with dead eyes while they deceived you, we've all encountered liars. Some lied out of fear, others out of habit, and the worst of them—the conscious deceivers—did it with strategy and confidence, like it was second nature.

We've seen how microexpressions, overcontrolled body language, and vague language can reveal the truth, even when the words don't. And when those signs are ignored, the consequences can be deep and painful, as people like Jenifer Faison learned the hard way. But here's what I want you to hold on to: Being lied to doesn't make you foolish; it makes you human. Let what you've learned in this chapter sharpen your instincts—not harden your heart. You have every right to protect yourself, but just remember: Staying aware doesn't mean staying closed off. You can keep your eyes open without keeping your heart locked shut.

***Let me ask you this: Have you ever struggled to stay away from a liar?***

*If you've ever gotten back together with your man after he cheated, or forgiven a friend who told a big, hurtful lie and kept them in your life, part of the reason is "Cognitive Dissonance." Cognitive dissonance is the mental discomfort a person experiences when they hold two or more conflicting beliefs, values, or attitudes. This psychological tension often arises when someone's actions don't align with their values. For instance, valuing honesty while being involved with someone who has lied. To reduce this discomfort, the mind looks for ways to resolve the inconsistency.*

*In the case of a liar, you might justify or downplay the lie ("It wasn't that serious"), rationalize the other person's behavior ("They were under a lot of stress"), or shift blame onto yourself ("Maybe I misunderstood"). These internal adjustments can make it easier to forgive the liar or even return to the relationship, not necessarily because trust has been rebuilt, but because maintaining the relationship feels easier than sitting with the tension of betrayal.*

*If you recently forgave your boyfriend again...swearing you know he's changed and will never do it again, know that your body might be telling a different story. Your nonverbal cues will likely reveal you are experiencing an inner conflict. You might show signs of discomfort through fidgeting, avoiding eye contact, mechanical smiles, or defensive body language like crossed arms or a tight posture. If you're trying to convince yourself or others that everything is fine, you might overcompensate by smiling too much, nodding excessively, or speaking in a tone that doesn't quite match your words. These subtle behaviors can signal that while you're saying you've forgiven the lie, your body is still expressing unease. In this way, cognitive dissonance doesn't just play out in the mind; it can be written all over your face and body.*

## CHAPTER SEVEN

# Command the Room

Back to those so-called flawless people who seem to radiate their own personal brand of sunshine. So confident and charismatic, dazzling yet warm, they can command the attention of an entire room with a simple adjustment of their nonverbal communication. Their eyes sparkle, their skin glows, they stand tall and proud, and their smile—a mix of kindness and subtle authority—leaves a lasting impression on everyone they meet. Every gesture they make and word they speak is delivered with poise and elegance like their perfect haircut with envy-inducing highlights. They have an innate ability to connect with people, making others feel seen and valued, drawing them in with their magical energy. They are never rattled or caught off guard, but ooze self-assurance in any situation. There's no ego here either—their flawlessness is not loud or overbearing, but gently potent, rooted in an unshakable sense of self. Sigh. I know. In the presence of one of these magnificent creatures it's easy to feel like a toad, isn't it? I'm going to let you in on something: This magic isn't about having extra confidence thanks to good genes, the best education, wealth, fame, or being tall with the right muscle mass either—these fine specimens of humanity know how to use their inner DJ to command the room.

DJs don't just play music. The best DJs are masters of energy, seamlessly reading the room and adjusting their set to control the crowd's emotions. With an instinctive feel for tempo, rhythm, and mood, they know when to build anticipation, when to drop a beat that electrifies the dance floor, and when to ease into a more hypnotic, sexy groove. Their ability to blend tracks, layer sounds, and time transitions perfectly keeps the energy flowing, making the audience feel as if they're on a shared journey. Whether hyping up a crowd with pulsating bass or creating an intimate moment with a soulful melody, top DJs command the vibe, shaping the atmosphere with every beat. The flawless ones take control of their immediate environment in the exact same way. And when you learn to control the energy of a room, you can command the exact outcome you want. The magic required to command a room is already in you; it's just a matter of unlocking it.

Commanding a room isn't just about having all heads turn toward you (although that's always nice, and often a natural reaction when you own the room); it's about *the feeling* you imprint on every single person present. Or to simply quote Maya Angelou, "People will forget what you said, people will forget what you did, but people will never forget how you made them feel." It's the ability to raise or lower the emotional temperature of a room through your body language alone—whether by walking in with calm, grounded confidence that settles a tense environment, or with vibrant energy that lifts and enlivens it.

Someone who commands the room and gets results knows how to use their head power zone to dial up the energy or take it down as needed. The head power zone refers to the area from the shoulders up, including your head, face, eyes, and neck—and it's the source of one of the most impactful tools in the nonverbal communication arsenal. This zone communicates presence, confidence, emotional intelligence, and authenticity before you ever say a word. It includes your eye contact, which can convey connection and credibility; your facial expressions, which reveal empathy, curiosity, or calm; and your head movements such as nodding, tilting, or remaining still, which show you're engaged, listening, and thoughtful.

Even the position of your neck and chin plays a role: A slightly lifted chin signals quiet confidence, while a dropped or tense head can be read as insecurity or hesitation. When used intentionally, the head power zone becomes a kind of nonverbal magnet, drawing others in and signaling that you're grounded, aware, and fully present. It's subtle, but it's what makes people lean in, feel seen, and remember how you made them feel. When you learn to take command of a space with your head power zone, you will attract opportunities, exude leadership skills, and develop an influential presence that will allow you to achieve anything.

Kim doesn't go to networking events to drink the nasty, overly sweet cocktails with her coworkers. Kim goes because she knows the room is full of opportunities that she wants to grab on to. As an example, when Kim attended one particular event, Kim didn't enter with a loud greeting or a dazzling outfit, though she looked effortlessly put-together as usual. It was her use of the head power zone that spoke volumes. From the moment she walked in, Kim made subtle but powerful choices. Her chin was slightly lifted—not arrogantly, but with quiet confidence. Her eyes scanned the room with calm curiosity, not desperation. She made genuine eye contact with people, held it just long enough to signal warmth and self-assurance, and then moved on, like a leader surveying the scene.

While her colleagues stuck together talking among themselves, Kim joined a small group conversation. She made sure to listen with her whole face. She wasn't waiting to talk; she was truly in the moment. She nodded slowly, brows rising with interest at the right moments, her mouth softening into a warm, real smile when someone shared something they were proud of. She lit up, not to perform, but to reflect back the energy of the speaker. All this made people feel seen.

When Kim did speak, she maintained an open posture (that's the heart power zone in action), often using her hands to emphasize points, capturing the attention of her listeners. Kim kept making the rounds, while her colleagues were still exactly where she left them (but they were watching her work the room with their jaws on the floor), and it wasn't long before she had charmed and impressed everyone present with her ability to listen, her astute conversational skills, and her confident but approachable personality.

Someone across the room noticed. Maybe it was the way people automatically leaned toward her when she spoke. Or how often laughter erupted around her, not because she was the loudest, but because she was the most present. That someone turned out to be the VP of a company Kim admired. The VP made her way over, almost on instinct. She'd picked up on Kim's energy before a single word was spoken. They chatted effortlessly, and Kim kept that head tilt of curiosity, that steady, open gaze that made others feel heard and respected. By the end of the night, the VP said, "We're actually looking for someone like you right now. Would you be open to chatting next week?" Boom. That's it. This kind of possibility exists in all kinds of rooms, all the time! If you know how to take command, the room opens up and the opportunities find *you*.

This is what happens when you understand how to utilize the head power zone. The head is one of the most powerful indicators of authority and influence. It serves as the control center of nonverbal communication, where facial expressions, eye contact, and head movements convey a full spectrum of leadership qualities…confidence, intelligence, credibility, attentiveness and assurance, empathy and warmth, and head movements like nodding or tilting that express active listening and engagement. Maintaining a level chin and steady gaze demonstrates composure and leadership, while avoiding excessive head tilting or darting eyes prevents signs of insecurity. A slight head nod can encourage engagement, while a raised eyebrow or firm gaze can assert dominance.

Leaders and successful individuals master the art of using their facial expressions with precision by remaining composed yet expressive enough to captivate their audience without appearing overly emotional or, worse, erratic. Sheryl Sandberg, former COO of Meta (Facebook) and author of *Lean In*, is a master when it comes to using the head power zone to command high-pressure environments. She isn't a brusque or domineering presence, but when she speaks, people listen. In interviews and on panels, Sandberg demonstrates centered, intentional head movements. She uses stillness strategically, keeping her head steady when listening to signal focus and groundedness. She doesn't fidget or overnod, which would suggest nervousness—no room for that in the pressure cooker boardrooms of Silicon Valley.

Instead, she offers slow, thoughtful nods that show she's actively engaged and taking others seriously. Whether she's addressing a crowd or answering a challenging question, she looks straight at the person or audience with a calm gaze… not a hard stare. That kind of eye contact projects clarity, presence, and trustworthiness.

Her facial expressions are another source of her strength. When others speak, she allows her emotions to register slight smiles, empathetic brow movements, softening her mouth when someone shares something vulnerable. It makes her appear human, rather than robotic. She shows she's listening not just with her ears, but with her whole face. She also uses micro-pauses before responding. These are characterized by moments of stillness that create space and draw people in. That brief delay signals, "I'm considering what you said." It's a subtle move, but incredibly effective. In male-dominated environments, she doesn't try to mimic loudness or posturing. Instead, she stays rooted in her own presence and the head power zone is central to that.

Utilizing the head power zone to own a room, like our girl Kim did, isn't about performance; it's about *presence.* It's the art of showing up with intention, grounded in who *you are*, and letting that confidence speak louder than any pitch. Kim's inner DJ was setting the tone—high energy, but not over-the-top. She executed the perfect vibe that let her stand out as her authentic self without trying too hard. When you align your nonverbal cues with genuine curiosity, respect, and self-assurance, like Kim did, *people respond.* Whether you're navigating a networking event, leading a team, or stepping into a new opportunity, your presence becomes your calling card. And when it's obvious you command the energy, everyone wants to be a part of it.

Just like Kim, just like Sheryl—it's not about being the loudest in the room. It's about being the most aware. And when you lead with that kind of awareness, rooms open, conversations deepen, and the right people find their way to you.

Activating the head power zone can also be your best approach when trying to dial down fears and uncertainty.

The quarterly town hall meeting was packed, way more than usual. Dozens of employees filled the room, some anxious, some skeptical, all waiting to hear how leadership planned to navigate the latest shake-up. Tension buzzed beneath the surface. Shoulders were stiff, and quiet murmurs were rippling through the crowd. At the front of the room, a few speakers had already tried to address the elephant in the room, but their rushed words and rigid body language only added to the unease. Then Isabelle stepped up. She didn't launch into a speech right away. She paused. She looked at the room—really looked. Her eyes scanned slowly and purposefully, making eye contact here and there, letting the silence settle like a deep breath. Her stance was grounded, spine tall but not stiff, and her hands rested loosely at her sides. Like a skilled DJ feeling the pulse of a packed dance floor, she knew the energy was too chaotic to push through; it needed to be gently tuned. Her voice, when she finally spoke, was low and melodic. Not flat, not dramatic—just steady. She let each sentence breathe. Her facial expressions were calm, almost meditative, signaling to the room, "You're safe. I'm not here to put a spin on things." She softened her gaze, kept her head still, and used intentional pauses, giving weight to her words and inviting the room to slow down with her.

And they did. Arms unfolded. Brows unknit. People leaned in. It was subtle, but the shift was real. She didn't sugarcoat the facts, but she delivered them with clarity and care. When someone raised a concern, she didn't interrupt or deflect; she nodded slowly, tilted her head just enough to show "I hear you," and responded with the same composed cadence. Her calm was contagious. By the end, the room wasn't just informed; they were grounded. Hopeful, even. And that wasn't because of what Isabelle said. It was how she said it. She'd tuned the frequency of the entire room with her nonverbal communication, guiding them out of chaos and back into connection.

After the meeting, conversations shifted. Instead of grumbling in corners, people stayed behind to share ideas, ask thoughtful questions, and reengage. The Big Boss, who had watched closely from the back of the room, approached Isabelle quietly afterward. "I don't know exactly what you just did," he said, "but you reset the entire tone of the room."

Two weeks later, Isabelle was asked to co-lead a new cross-functional task force—one that required not just intelligence, but presence. She hadn't asked for it. She hadn't campaigned. She simply showed up with the kind of calm, grounded energy people follow. That's the kind of influence that can't be faked. It's earned, in the silence between words, in the space you create, and in how others feel when you're in command of the room.

Isabelle was able to command an entire room of anxious and even angry people because she deliberately used the head power zone to signal trust; she wanted people to feel safe, seen, and connected rather than antagonistic. She grounded herself before she even spoke. Her feet were planted firmly, her posture tall but relaxed, shoulders down and open...immediately signaling calm, centered authority. She let the room settle before activating the head power zone, scanning the space with slow, purposeful eye contact that connected with individuals, not just the crowd. Her gaze wasn't rushed or performative; it was steady and curious, saying, "I've got you." Even her head movements were intentional: utilizing the "Nurturing Nod"… the slow, intentional head movement that says, "I'm listening." She wasn't performing calm; she was actually calm. And the room followed her.

Isabelle's calm, collected influence is not unlike Satya Nadella's, one of the most respected and quietly powerful leaders of this generation. When Satya Nadella became CEO of Microsoft in 2014, he didn't enter with bold proclamations or power plays. Instead, he brought something far more radical for a tech giant: humility, emotional intelligence, and unwavering composure. And that calmness wasn't just internal—it was broadcast through every aspect of his nonverbal communication.

Nadella speaks in a soft, even tone. He doesn't raise his voice to fill the room and get attention, yet people lean in. Why? Because he combines his words with body language that signals, "I'm here, I'm listening, I'm steady." He often uses long pauses, not as a tactic, but as a natural part of his cadence. This creates space for others to process, reflect, and contribute. It also gives his words weight because he doesn't overuse them.

When he's onstage or in meetings, his posture is open and relaxed. He doesn't fidget or use expansive gestures to dominate attention. Instead, he gestures with intention—measured hand movements that emphasize points, not distract from them. His facial expressions are neutral but warm, making others feel safe enough to share ideas, challenge norms, or ask questions. Much like Isabelle, Nadella's quiet authority stems from deep listening. He makes direct, calm eye contact, often tilting his head slightly when someone speaks, a nonverbal cue of genuine interest. He rarely interrupts. He lets people finish so they feel seen, heard, and respected. And that changes the dynamic of any room he enters.

In transforming Microsoft's culture, Nadella didn't rely on force or charisma. He used presence, patience, and empathy—anchored by masterful control of the head power zone. Just like Isabelle, he didn't come in trying to dominate a space. He came in ready to tune it.

When you practice these nonverbal techniques until they become second nature, you'll take command of any space with effortless control. No second-guessing, no overthinking, just pure, magnetic presence. You'll have the ability to dial up the energy, electrifying a room and drawing people toward you; or slow it down, creating intimacy and intrigue with a single glance or subtle touch. Mastering this means you're no longer at the mercy of chance or luck. When you're in charge of the energy and the attention, ultimately that means getting exactly what you want.

Baby, that also means your days of being subject to someone else's whims and demands are over! Never again will you look at another woman's achievements and think, "Part of that must be luck." When you understand that *you* have the power to alter the energy of the room with NVC, your life will open up before you like a field of flowing lavender. You'll be able to naturally uplift spirits and inspire others with enthusiasm and optimism, making people feel engaged and inspired. You'll be able to conjure up a dynamic vibe in a snap that creates a sense of momentum for everyone around you. Having total control, nothing will faze you. You'll be able to handle any situation by fine-tuning the energy you need on demand, melting chaos into calmness, or even transforming fear into determination. All with the power *in your body*. This isn't about being a miracle maker; it's about knowing how to use your NVC to command the vibe of the room so you can get what you want. All you have to do is get out there where everything is yours for the taking.

**_Let me ask you this:_**
**_How do you wrap your package?_**

*Momma Bird used to say, "You can't make a million bucks if you look like you were born in the dollar store." While I'm a full-fledged believer in the power of nonverbal communication, you've still got to wrap your package right if you want to dominate in business or in life. You cannot come off as a Basic. If you show up wearing an ill-fitting, bargain-basement cardigan over a stretched-out T-shirt with a pair of cheap slacks that don't fit your body right, you are doing yourself a disservice. Your overall style needs to read as FIERCE, and you need to be honest with yourself about the image you are projecting.*

*The way you look, from your clothes to your grooming and posture, sends powerful messages that can influence how others perceive your competence, confidence, and professionalism. Ensuring that your package looks good is about aligning your outward appearance with the image you want to project with your nonverbal communication. Show your style, baby. I'm not asking you to spend a fortune on clothes, but I am asking you to be intentional about what's in your closet. A well-curated wardrobe isn't about having more; it's about having better. A small collection of quality pieces that fit well, flatter your shape, and align with your personal style will always serve you more. When you invest in pieces that make you feel confident and put-together, getting dressed becomes effortless, and your presence carries an extra energy that boosts your self-assurance and feeling of refinement even higher.*

*When you take the time to look polished and put-together, you communicate that you respect yourself and the people you interact with. It shows that you're mindful of the context you're in and that you take your role or responsibilities seriously. When you look good, you carry yourself with more self-assurance, which in turn makes others perceive you as more competent and capable. Wrapping your package isn't about following superficial fashion standards; it's about adding additional support to the nonverbal message you send out into the world. When your style reflects your ambition, confidence, and professionalism, you set yourself up for success by commanding respect and leaving a positive, lasting impression. So please, clean out that closet if need be.*

## CHAPTER EIGHT

# How to Get Attention (Without Saying a Word)

Now we're going to tackle the subject I get asked about all the time from women of all different ages and backgrounds... MEN.[1] Let's get something straight from the jump. Getting a quality man—whether it's THE man, your man, or just a man *for now* isn't about contorting yourself into someone else's idea of perfection. It's not about duck lips or blown-out hair or wearing heels that make your feet cry mercy. It's about energy. Specifically, the kind you project without ever opening your mouth. Baby, your nonverbal communication (NVC, if you're nasty) is already speaking volumes, whether you're single, taken, or somewhere in between, sipping wine and weighing your options while you look at engagement rings on Instagram.

1. I'm speaking directly to my men here. Do not make the mistake of thinking this chapter doesn't apply to you and skip over it. I haven't forgotten about y'all. There's some essential information in here for you too.

The good news? You can take your NVC and dial it up, shape it, play with it, and turn it into a full-body frequency that says, "I am magnetic, and yes, I know it." This isn't about being perfect. It's about being alluring. And let me tell you, alluring is so much better than perfect. Take the queen of the gap-toothed gaze, for example. French actress, singer, and former face of Chanel Vanessa Paradis is the textbook definition of *effortless allure*. Her tooth gap is iconic, not something she hid or "fixed," but something that became part of her charm. Her beauty isn't flawless in a cookie-cutter way; it's *undeniably hers*. She speaks softly, moves slowly, and has that classic French ability to make you feel like you're the only person in the room. Now *that's* power.

Auntie Linda needs you to hear this—so just in case you're still holding on to the idea that seduction requires soft curves, big lashes, and some Barbie-approved symmetry, allow me to gently shatter that myth—with cheekbones. Enter: Tilda Swinton. Tilda is not your classic girl next door. She's not your Victoria's Secret pinup. She is something else entirely, and that's what makes her absolutely hypnotic. She's tall, angular, pale as moonlight, and carries herself like she just floated in from a planet where elegance is currency and nobody raises their voice. Her look is striking—sharp features, a statuesque frame, and androgyny that somehow feels more sensual than overt femininity. And she doesn't hide any of it. She leans all the way in.

What makes Tilda so alluring isn't that she fits a mold; it's that she refuses to. Her movements are deliberate. Her gaze is precise. She knows the power of stillness better than most actors working today. In interviews, she often pauses before speaking, and when she does speak, her voice is soft, deliberate, and wrapped in mystery. It's like every word is an offering—not because she's trying to be sexy, but because you feel as if you're hearing a fairy goddess from another realm speak, and it's magical.

Watch this woman on the red carpet. No frantic posing, no teeth-baring grin. She stands. She glides. She tilts her head ever so slightly. Her body language says, "Go ahead, you can look as long as you want"—and then it's like she disappears into the mist.

Another great example is Ayo Edebiri. Here's a woman who isn't trying to be anyone's version of polished perfection and that's exactly what makes her so magnetic. She doesn't float in like a fantasy; she walks in like she belongs, sharp, witty, and humming with intelligence. Her beauty is subtle but unforgettable—a charmingly crooked smile, expressive eyes that flicker with what you imagine to be twelve thoughts at once. She doesn't seduce with softness; instead, she charms with her sincerity. Ayo's allure lies in how real she is. She doesn't perform femininity; she redefines it. She's cutely awkward and grounded, quick-witted and unbothered, and somehow manages to pull off deadpan like it's a superpower. There's a confidence in the quiet that feels subversive in all the best ways. Watch her in *The Bear*. She doesn't try to steal scenes—she just occupies them with poise. Whether she's holding her ground in the kitchen or reacting with microexpressions so precise they could slice through steel, Ayo is always in control of her space. Her body language says, "I don't need your approval—I've got things to do." She stands like a woman who's carried every version of herself into the room and doesn't regret a single one.

Ayo doesn't chase the spotlight. She earns it with wit, presence, and a refusal to be anyone but herself, and she reminds us that power doesn't have to shout. Sometimes, it just raises an eyebrow. And that is when you know you're in the presence of someone unforgettable.

Vanessa, Tilda, and Ayo are all proof that allure isn't about blending in—it's about owning the space you were born to take up. They turn so-called imperfections into their own brand of beauty. Unapologetically. And that, darling, is what makes people crave more—otherworldly, unbothered, and totally unforgettable.

Let's get one thing clear: You don't need to perform, chase, or shape-shift to catch a man's attention. You just need to know how to show up—not with noise, but *with presence.* And your best asset in the game of attraction? Your nonverbal communication. Yes, Queen. It's not about your eyeliner, your outfit, or your push-up bra. It's how you move, how you look at someone, and the energy you bring into a space. Because allure doesn't scream. It whispers. And when you get the whisper right, men will be flocking to you.

Now let's not pretend this is just for the single ladies. Married women, I see you too. You've still got it, and if you feel like you've lost it somewhere between the big career, laundry, and school pickup, I'm here to help you "reactivate." For a married woman, "reactivating" means reigniting that quiet fire within, not by reinventing herself, but by returning to her natural allure, the kind that may have gotten buried under carpool schedules and sporting equipment. It's about using nonverbal communication to shift the dynamic silently. Think walking into the room with intention, not exhaustion (not easy, I know, but do your best). Making eye contact that lingers, not out of duty, but desire. It's about slowing movements just enough to be noticed—the brush of an arm as you pass by. All this lets your body language say, "I still see you, and I want to be seen too."

Reactivating isn't about seduction in a movie-scene way—I mean, seriously, we all know that pile of dishes in the kitchen isn't sexy, but you've got to forget about that; they'll still be there later. Instead, this is about reclaiming presence, owning energy, and remembering that flirtation doesn't stop at "I do." Sometimes it just needs a little invitation to come back to life.

My friend Danielle demonstrated how this works beautifully. She'd been with her husband for over a decade. Things weren't bad, but the spark was…dim. One night, I suggested she try something simple. Instead of her usual post-dinner zombie shuffle to the couch to watch Netflix until they both fell asleep, she tried something different. She walked into the living room slowly, eyes on him, no rush. She smiled—not big, but slow and knowing. She ran one hand gently along her neck, like she was thinking, but she wasn't. She was directing energy. He looked up from his phone and blinked like he'd just remembered she was a goddess. Ten minutes later, they were making out in the kitchen like teenagers. Same hoodie with the same ketchup stain. Same ponytail. Different energy. She didn't say a word. Later on, she described the scene to me as "hotter than the fire in a Japanese restaurant's hibachi grill."

A woman named Marisol once told me about a first date that started out lukewarm until she decided to lean into her body language and try my technique "Barely There Flirtation." Barely there flirtation is the art of seduction in its most subtle, refined form, like a whisper that lingers just long enough to make someone turn their head. It's not about making a move; it's about creating the possibility of one. A flicker of eye contact that holds for one heartbeat too long before drifting away, a smile that plays at the corners of your mouth mid-conversation, a soft laugh as you lean in just slightly closer than necessary. It's the brush of a hand that feels accidental but isn't, the tilt of your head that invites curiosity, not commitment. The magic of barely there flirtation is that it never tries too hard; it lives in the spaces between words, the pauses that say, "I'm intrigued, but I could vanish at any moment." It's not about declaring interest; it's about suggesting it, then letting their imagination do the rest.

Marisol's chemistry with Lucas, a hot guy she had been in a mutual flirtation with for a few weeks at the dog park, was palpable. Their conversations flowed easily, and they had a lot in common, but when they finally went out on a date (without their dogs), things were a little strained. Marisol said to get things going she "stopped focusing on the conversation and started feeling him instead." She dropped her voice just a touch, let her eye contact linger a heartbeat longer than usual, and tilted her shoulder toward him when she laughed. No dramatic moves.

Just small, intentional shifts. At one point, she accidentally-on-purpose let her fingers brush his when she reached for her glass. He flinched—like he'd just been zapped (in a good way)—and from then on, his entire body leaned toward hers.

At the end of the night, he said, "I can't stop looking at you." That's the magic of the barely there move. It's not about taking over. It's about inviting someone in and letting the rest unfold naturally. Make sure you take those dogs out first, though; you won't want any interruptions.

My friend Talia swears she met her fiancé because of the seductive handshake, which I've shown to countless women over the years. The seductive handshake is all about confidence, subtlety, and just the right amount of intention. You start by approaching slowly, with relaxed posture and soft eye contact. As you extend your hand, keep your fingers open and your palm warm, not stiff. When your hands connect, give a gentle but confident grip, just enough pressure to feel present, not overpowering. Let your thumb softly graze the back of their hand and hold the shake a beat longer than usual. Maintain eye contact, then release slowly with a slight, knowing smile. It's not just a greeting—it's a moment.

At a work event, she was introduced to a man from another advertising agency. He was tall, reserved, and she could not get over how annoyingly good-looking this man was. Before even thinking about it, she extended her hand with slow confidence, gave a firm but warm grip, and let her thumb gently glide across the back of his hand. The contact lasted a fraction longer than necessary, and she locked eyes the whole time. "He didn't let go," she told me, laughing. "He just stood there, holding my hand like I was a rare artifact." That night, he asked to walk her to her car. Two years later, he slipped a two-carat, nearly flawless diamond ring on that hand. That's what I call a return on investment.

Jasmine, a woman I met at one of my body language seminars, shared how she used my "Oh-So-Juicy Lip" move during a museum date (yes, classy!). The oh-so-juicy lip move is a subtle, seductive gesture that draws attention to your lips without saying a thing. Start with soft, relaxed eye contact. Keep your lips parted just slightly, then gently bite or graze your lower lip, slow and light, nothing dramatic. Hold the pose for a second, then release with a slow, playful smile. It's suggestive without being obvious (they were in a museum, after all), creating just enough tension to make them wonder what kind of sexy thought you might be thinking...and wishing you'd say it.

There's a reason biting your lip works: It's primal. But it has to be subtle. Think whisper, not billboard. While standing in front of a painting, she caught her date staring—not at the priceless work of art, but at her. So she softly bit her lower lip, paused, and then looked back at the painting like nothing happened. "I saw him physically lean toward me," she said. "Like he was trying to figure me out." He later admitted that moment short-circuited his brain. "I couldn't even remember the name of the artist," he told her. That's the power of a single, silent moment.

Neck and collarbone touches are so underestimated. Subtle, feminine, and full of sensual tension—and wildly effective because they draw attention to one of the most delicate, vulnerable parts of the body. A slow, casual graze of the collarbone or a gentle touch to the neck signals softness, self-awareness, and quiet confidence. It's not a show; it's an invitation. The movement feels natural, almost absentminded, but it speaks volumes: "I'm comfortable in my skin, and you're lucky to be this close to it."

Case in point: my girlfriend Serena, at a wedding. She was mid-conversation with the groom's cousin when she adjusted her necklace...slowly, fingers brushing her collarbone, eyes still on him. She didn't even realize she'd done it. *He did.* He asked for her number before dessert was served. Later, he told her, "You did this thing with your hand and your neck, and it was...I don't know, elegant." Elegant? Sure, but it's not that simple. That gesture rewired his frontal cortex because it hit all the right neurological pleasure points: subtle vulnerability, unspoken confidence, and just enough sensual tension to spark his imagination into overdrive.

The neck and collarbone are also primal zones—intimate, exposed, and rich with nerve endings our brains are hardwired to notice. When she touched her collarbone slowly, effortlessly, like it was second nature, his subconscious clocked it as softness, sensuality, and mystery. And the girl wasn't even trying! This move wasn't just "elegant"; it was chemical, releasing dopamine and hijacking rational thought. She flipped a switch with one simple move, and that poor man didn't stand a chance.

You don't need to have legs like Tina Turner to use them to make a man swoon, by the way. Pulling off this showstopping and sexy maneuver is all about grace and control. Sit up tall with your shoulders relaxed and your core engaged. Then, slowly—and I mean slowly—cross one leg over the other in a fluid, deliberate motion. Let your top foot gently rest, do not dangle as if it fell asleep and you're trying to wake it up, and angle your body slightly toward the person you want to engage. Add a soft gaze or slight smile, and boom—you've just turned a simple seated pose into a full-body flirtation. You've seen the woman who crosses her legs and suddenly everyone in the room tunes in like she's the main character. That could be you.

My client Camille learned this the fun way. She was sitting across from her date, mid-convo, when she shifted, slowly, purposefully, crossing one leg over the other and subtly angling her body toward him. She didn't say anything. But he leaned in, eyes lower than before. She didn't even finish her glass of wine before he said, "I don't know what it is, but I can't stop looking at you." It was the leg cross. The power move that never fails.

Finally, "the Alluring Lean-In," which is easy to execute and oh, so unforgettable. This move is all about timing, intention, and just the right amount of closeness. Start with open body language, shoulders relaxed, posture soft. When the moment feels right, slowly lean in toward the other person, closing the space just enough to create intimacy *without invading*. Keep your eyes on theirs, and if you want to dial it up, add a slight head tilt or a soft smile. Hold the moment for a beat before you speak or pull back. The magic is in that pause. It builds tension, invites connection, and makes the moment feel like a secret between just you two.

Let me tell you about Leah. She met someone at a conference we were both speaking at. They'd been chatting, and the energy was solid, but a little flat. Then, mid-sentence, Leah leaned in just a few inches, enough to close the gap, but not enough to invade and freak the poor man out. Her eyes stayed soft, her head tilted slightly, her voice dropped just a hair. Boom. Chemistry activated. He later told her he wasn't even sure what had happened in that moment. He was too distracted by her mesmerizing energy and how close she felt, like the rest of the room had faded away, leaving just the two of them. Now that's how you seduce with presence, not performance.

This is very important. Every story here has one thing in common: These women didn't try too hard. They didn't script their lines, hike their skirts, or bat their lashes like a cartoon character. They tuned in to their own energy and turned it up just enough to be felt, not flaunted. This is your reminder that you already have everything you need to attract the right kind of attention. You don't need to be louder. You need to be more you. More present. More intentional. More alluring. So, walk into the room like you designed the vibe. Smile like you know a secret. Cross your legs like it's a slow dance. And remember: The most irresistible woman in the room is the one who knows she doesn't have to say much...because her body already did.

## A NOTE TO MY SINGLE MEN: THIS IS HOW YOU GET YOURSELF A QUEEN

Ask any woman, and she'll say the worst thing a man can do if he's interested in a woman isn't to reek of cologne (but avoid that, please) but to reek of entitlement. Women have had our space invaded without an invitation, we've been talked at instead of to…and some of you men mistake your persistence for charm. Guess what? It's not charming. Oh, there are so many ways to kill the vibe before you even say hello, but if we had to crown the worst offender? It's desperation disguised as dominance. Picture this: He puffs up his chest like a cartoon gym rat, spreads his limbs across three chairs like he owns the place, and locks eyes like he's trying to burn holes through her soul. Sir, this is not an alpha move—it's giving overcompensating energy with a side of creep. Women are hardwired to clock threat versus safety in a heartbeat, and that aggressive posturing screams, "I need validation," not "I'm worth your time."

A close second? Nervous, scattered energy. If he's fidgeting with his sleeves, checking his phone every thirty seconds, or bouncing his knee like he's on a caffeine bender, it signals insecurity and discomfort. No woman wants to play emotional support animal for a stranger at a social event. Confidence is calm. Stillness. Presence. If his body is screaming, "Anywhere but here," her instinct will be to follow that same exit strategy. Bottom line? If he's not grounded in himself, she won't feel safe enough to be curious. And that door will close real quick. So instead of showing up like one giant ego, let Auntie Linda show you how to connect with a person rather than acting like you're trying to win a prize at a carnival.

First, please forget pickup lines. Those are for sitcoms. If you really want to catch a woman's eye, it's not about what you say; it's about what your body broadcasts. Confidence doesn't need a microphone. If you walk in like you know who you are but don't need to prove it to anyone? That's magnetic. We're talking smooth, grounded strides like your shoes cost money and your mama raised you right. Shoulders back, chest open, and eyes that scan the room like you are both alert and unbothered. Bonus points if you give off that unspoken "I'm here because I want to be, not because I need to impress you" energy. That's CEO-level swagger and trust me, women notice. But here's the real secret sauce: microexpressions. That tiny upturn of the mouth when you catch her eye? The quick eyebrow flash that says, "I see you, and I like what I see"? That's better than any one-liner. And let's not forget the power of stillness. A man who isn't jittery, fidgeting, or peacocking like a caffeinated rooster sends one very clear signal: "I'm secure. I'm grounded. I'm not chasing—I'm choosing." And that calm assurance? Whew. It's not just attractive; it's addictive.

And where you position yourself in a room says just as much as how you stand. A man who gets it doesn't hover in the shadows or post up by the bar like he's waiting to be summoned. No, he chooses a spot with purpose. Maybe he leans casually against a doorway, owning the space without blocking it, inviting but not desperate. Maybe he positions himself just a few feet from the center of action, close enough to observe, far enough away to stay mysterious. That's strategy, babe. He's not crowding anyone's energy. He's pulling it. And when it comes to engaging her? He angles his body just enough to show interest without cornering her like it's a hostage negotiation. One foot slightly turned toward her, torso open, keeping her in his line of sight without laser-beaming his eyes straight at her like she's prey. That body angle says, "I'm interested, not intrusive." Women pick up on that nuance immediately. It's the difference between "Ugh, another one," and "Wait…who is he?" Because the man who understands positioning isn't chasing attention—he's commanding curiosity. And that, my friend, is irresistible.

## A NOTE TO MY MARRIED MEN: HOW TO KEEP THINGS SAUCY WITH YOUR QUEEN

A married man who really knows his wife doesn't wait for date night or a vacation to turn on the charm—he seduces with subtlety, and he does it on a random Tuesday. It simply starts with presence. When you walk into the room and actually see her… don't just glance at her while you're checking your emails. Use your whole body and shift toward her. You want those shoulders square, the phone down, and eye contact that lingers a second longer than necessary. That gaze says, "You still stop me in my tracks." And oh, that alone can send shivers down her spine. Add in a confident stroll across the living room, no rush, no flinch, just calm control, and maybe a hand on her lower back while you lean in to whisper something private, and boom: A discussion about the monthly budget is suddenly not the priority anymore.

But it's not just what you do; it's how you hold yourself. When you move with intention, unhurried, grounded, and just a little closer than usual—you are creating a current. A gentle touch at the waist while passing by, your voice dropping a half-octave when you say her name, a playful smirk when she least expects it…these are what light the sparks. It's the nonverbal way of saying, "I still choose you. And I still want you." When you can make your wife feel like the most desirable woman in the world while she's wearing sweatpants and hunting for lost keys, that's not just seduction; it's like falling in love all over again.

***Let me ask you this:***
***Do you debrief yourself after a date?***

*After a mission, CIA officers don't just grab a drink and move on. They debrief, and they are meticulous about it. They sit down, go over the facts, assess the atmosphere, dissect body language, and identify what worked, what didn't, and what nearly got them killed. The goal? To get sharper for next time. Every twitch, pause, or glance might hold valuable intelligence, and nothing is left to chance.*

*Now imagine applying that same discipline to your dating life. No, you're not decoding nuclear secrets, but you are gathering valuable intelligence—on yourself, your date, and the connection (or the lack thereof) that just played out across a candlelit table or during that awkward sidewalk goodbye. The key? Do a "post-date nonverbal debrief." Ask yourself:*

- *How did I enter the room? Was I rushed or grounded?*
- *Did I make solid eye contact or stare at the menu like it had the answers to the mysteries of the universe?*
- *Was I fidgeting or relaxed with my heart power zone open and activated?*
- *Did I smile with sincerity or default to my "polite but dead inside" face?*
- *Did I play a positive role in keeping the conversation going?*

- *Did I execute any of Auntie Linda's moves, and if so, what was the result?*

*You're not beating yourself up—you're being self-reflective and analyzing your own signal system. Maybe your arms were crossed the whole time and you didn't even notice. Maybe you leaned back too much and seemed disengaged or leaned in too early and came off overly eager. Did you mirror their body language at all, or did you unintentionally create distance?*

*CIA officers don't wait for external feedback; they learn by watching the tapes, reviewing posture, tone, and timing. You can do the same (but please do not videotape your dates). The more aware you become of the energy you bring into the room, the more you can fine-tune it. Eventually, your body becomes your best wingman, sending the exact message you meant to send, without you having to overthink it. And hey, maybe the date wasn't "the one." But that doesn't mean it was a waste. You just gathered intel, and next time you'll walk in smarter, smoother, and more aligned with the story your body's telling.*

## CHAPTER NINE

# The Power of Positioning

Let's set the scene: You walk into a room. It could be a networking event, a party, a conference, a dinner—you name it. Where do you go? Straight to the snack table to distract yourself with a plate of sushi? Tuck yourself into the corner with your phone? Find other terrified people to spend the evening with, silently? Slide next to your friend and become their human barnacle for the rest of the evening? All you lifeboaters and lurkers out there? You might want to have a highlighter handy for this chapter; I promise it will help you.

If your first instinct is to hide, it's okay—we've all been there. But it's time to stop fading into the furniture. Because here's the truth: Where you place yourself in a room says everything about your confidence, energy, and what you believe you deserve. And guess what? People read it instantly and make decisions accordingly. You don't have to say a word, but if your body is sending "I'm not sure I belong here" energy, the room picks it up and reflects it right back to you: "If that person doesn't belong, then I definitely don't need to bother talking to them."

High-powered people don't go to events to hang out with the B team; they are there to make the most of the room—to make contacts, gain opportunities, and level up their careers. Ever wonder why the server with the tray of champagne never makes it to you? She might sense you don't think you deserve any! Let's fix this sad situation now and forever. When you know how to position yourself correctly within a space, physically and energetically, you become the kind of person people notice without knowing why. You're magnetic. Not brash. Not overbearing. Just present and establishing yourself as someone worth noting.

Let me tell you about Liv. Liv used to enter rooms like she was apologizing for existing. She'd hover by the wall, stare at her drink like it was a crystal ball, and wait for someone, anyone, to approach her. (Spoiler alert: They rarely did.) One night, after a lovingly blunt pep talk from yours truly, Liv tried something different. She walked into an art opening solo, took two slow steps into the room, and paused. She scanned the space, not frantically like she'd melt into a puddle if she didn't find someone she knew, but with a calm curiosity. Then she planted herself not near the exit, not by the bar (remember, that's a beginner move for breaking barriers, and now we are on to advanced tactics), but in the "natural flow of the room," just left of center, close to a high-top table, facing outward.

The natural flow of the room reveals itself through a mix of movement, energy, and connection. Watch where people are naturally gathering. Are there conversational clusters forming in the center, near the host, or by the windows? Are there certain areas people pass through quickly versus spaces where they linger? Notice the "gravitational pull" of the room, where eye contact, laughter, and body orientation seem to point. These cues reveal the path of energy, where influence and interaction are naturally flowing. Step into that stream and go with the flow, baby; do not try to move against it. You want to position yourself near, but not crowding, the high-energy zones, close enough to be part of the action, but with just enough space to move with intention.

Once she found her position, she stood tall, let her shoulders drop, unclenched her jaw, and softened her eyes. She didn't say a word. Within a few minutes, a man approached her to compliment her boots (girlfriend has style). Within ten, two women had asked if they knew her from somewhere. By the end of the night, Liv had made three solid connections—one of whom turned out to be a gallery curator who offered to look at her portfolio. Why? Because Liv had stopped hiding in the shadows and placed herself in the current of the room's energy.

Your physical location is like a silent broadcast that announces: Are you open? Are you grounded? Are you worth approaching? (You are, obviously—but others need to feel it.) And then, there's your body. The way you hold yourself once you've chosen your spot is everything.

Take Casey, a young woman I've come to know since repeatedly meeting her at conferences. Casey always showed up to events looking amazing—impeccable hair, killer heels, the whole vibe—but she never made a real connection. Why? Because she picked a position on the sidelines and even worse, her posture screamed, "Do not disturb." Arms folded, legs crossed away from the action, head down. A walking fortress in designer boots.

So one night, we tried an experiment. At her next event, Casey walked in, picked a visible spot—not front and center, but not tucked in a corner as usual either—and adopted what I call a posture of "elevated ease." She stood with her feet shoulder width apart, one hand gently holding her drink, the other free. Chin lifted. Body open. She let her gaze wander, slowly taking in the room without looking like she was searching for anyone. And when someone caught her eye? She held it. Just for a beat. That hold was like sending a direct message... "Why don't you come my way for a chat?"

By the end of the night, Casey was deep in conversation with two fascinating people, one of whom later became her mentor. All because she switched up her positioning and stopped crossing her arms like a gate and started using her presence like a key that can open any door. Let's be clear: This is not about performance. It's about intention. You're not pretending to be someone else because you don't need to be someone else! You're allowing the most magnetic version of you to step forward into the natural flow of the room.

Ariaya, whom I'd known for years, was going through a divorce, feeling all kinds of invisible, and reluctantly went to a friend's dinner party. She told me later, "I was ready to disappear the moment I walked in." But instead of hiding in the kitchen, she took a deep breath, walked into the living room, and sat on the arm of a chair, upright, comfortable, and open to the room. This is "the Elevated Anchor," an easy-to-execute approach that works for any event that's held in a living room, or at parties, or casual mixers. Skip the couch and take a perch on an armrest or a barstool; even standing with one hand resting lightly on a high-top works. Elevation catches the eye. It positions you as someone active and engaged instead of slouched or sunk into the furniture.

After selecting her perch, she crossed one leg slowly, let her body relax, and engaged with whoever sat nearby. She didn't flirt. She didn't force it. She simply took up a little more space than usual. By the end of the night, not only had she made a few new friends, but her friend's cousin—tall, bearded, with deep dimples—asked her out for coffee the next day. When she asked him what made him come over, he said, "You looked like you were exactly where you wanted to be."

Taking up space in a room where people are gathered is important because it signals that you belong there. It's not about being physically overbearing or spreading yourself out, as if you're testing out a new mattress; it's about owning your presence with confidence and intention. When you take up space, you communicate self-assurance, approachability, and status without saying a word. People subconsciously read your posture, your stillness, and your comfort level. Shrinking yourself by hunching, tucking in, or hovering at the edges sends the message that you're unsure or unimportant, even if that's not how you feel inside. But when you claim your space—planting your feet, opening your posture, and making calm eye contact—you create a magnetic field around you. Others are more likely to engage with you, take you seriously, and remember you. In rooms filled with power dynamics and subtle social hierarchies, how you physically exist in the space can quietly elevate your influence.

So next time you enter a space, ask yourself: "Am I in the room, or am I watching from the sidelines?"; "Am I taking up space with intention, or shrinking myself to be polite?" Because confidence doesn't shout. It doesn't stomp. It doesn't demand. It places itself calmly in the room and then waits for the world to catch up.

"The Triangle Technique" is a quiet power move that makes you instantly more magnetic and socially generous, because there are times when we need to help another soul out. Here's how it works: When you're talking to someone, instead of facing them dead-on like you're in an interview, angle your body slightly open—creating space for a third person to join. This nonverbal cue says, "There's room here," but without you looking sad and desperate for someone to talk to. It's simply an invitation, and people will take you up on it.

Take Maya, for example. She was chatting with a colleague at a fundraiser when she noticed someone hovering nearby, clearly interested in joining the conversation but unsure how. Instead of tightening the circle, Maya subtly shifted her stance, angled her shoulders, and smiled at the newcomer. Boom, triangle formed. Within seconds, the conversation expanded, and the energy shifted from polite small talk to genuine connection. The best part? That third person turned out to be the editor of a major lifestyle magazine (although the woman clearly needs to up her game in the NVC department). Three weeks later, Maya's business was featured in a full-page spread. All because she left the door open, literally with her body, and was generous enough to let others in.

### ROOM MAPPING

Here's a technique I use whenever possible that can put the most heightened nerves at ease. Room mapping is the subtle, strategic art of reading a room before you make your move. It's not dramatic. No binoculars or spy gadgets required. It's simply taking a beat to assess the social, energetic, and physical layout of the space the moment you arrive or, even better, before, should the opportunity present itself. I've been known to check out rooms where I'm speaking to get the lay of the land the day before my event is scheduled. When you "map" a room, you're looking for things like this:

- Where is the energy concentrated? That's where group clustering happens—often signaled by laughter, happy chatting, and a positive vibe.
- Who's holding court? That's the person others are orbiting or subtly facing and looking at.
- Where are the dead zones? Corners, walls, and areas where people are disengaged or passing through. And can you please stay out of the servers' way too?

- What are the traffic patterns? Where are people walking, lingering, or naturally drifting?

Room mapping lets you make intentional choices instead of reactive ones. Instead of defaulting to the nearest wall or awkwardly chasing a tray of mini quiches, you step into the flow of the room more easily, placing yourself in high-energy zones, near influential people, or at conversational intersections. It's a powerful move because it tells the room you're not just present; you're perceptive. And perceptiveness? That's one of the sexiest, most magnetic forms of intelligence there is.

You've walked into the room with intention. You've claimed your space like the main character you are. But now what? You've got to sit somewhere, right? Ahh yes, the humble seat, a modest piece of furniture that's charged with meaning. Make no mistake, where you sit and whom you sit next to are wildly underestimated parts of your nonverbal game. And if you think seating doesn't matter, let me gently ask: Do you want to be remembered, or do you want to blend in with the upholstery?

Let's start by talking about the conference table, that sacred rectangle (or terrifying oval) where promotions, projects, power dynamics, your salary, and your future vacation days are quietly decided. Most people default to what's safe: mid-table, somewhere in the cluster, hands folded like they're waiting to be dismissed. But if you want to be seen by everyone who matters, you need to be strategic. If you're new to the room or not leading the meeting, don't go full alpha and sit at the head. That can read as tone-deaf or just awkward. Instead, aim for a "seat adjacent to power." Sit one or two chairs away from the person running the show. That spot puts you in their line of sight and their orbit, without overstepping. It says, "I'm engaged, aware, and ready." You're not hovering in the background waiting to be called on. You're in the mix.

Now, let's talk money, honey—as in that moment you ask for a raise, a promotion, or the project of your dreams. You've prepped. You've practiced. You've even done the power pose in the bathroom beforehand (yes, it works). But here's a little trick from the body language gods: Sit to the left of the person you're negotiating with. Yes, you read that right. Sit to their left. Why? Because of how our brains are wired. The left visual field is processed by the brain's right hemisphere, which is more tuned in to emotion, empathy, and connection. When you sit to someone's left, they're more likely to feel aligned with you, to hear what you're saying in a more favorable light, and to view you less as a threat and more as a trusted partner. It's subtle, psychological judo—and it works.

Let me give you a real-life story. My client Hannah was gearing up to ask her boss for a bump in title and salary. She had all the receipts: performance wins, glowing feedback, the spreadsheet to end all spreadsheets. I gave her one last tip: "Sit to his left." She raised an eyebrow, but she did it. She walked in, greeted him warmly, and chose the chair to his immediate left—not across from him, not directly next to the door. The energy shifted immediately. Instead of an oppositional vibe, it felt like they were on the same team, looking at the future together. She made her case calmly, clearly, and he said yes. Not in a month, not after budget reviews. Right then. She called me afterward and said, "I don't know if it was the chair or the spreadsheet, but either way…I got the title and the money." Baby, it was the chair.

Have you ever been to an event where there is a legit celebrity present? You're dying to talk to the famous reporter, the bestselling author, the CEO who is a household name. You are psyching yourself up for an approach, but here's the problem: So is everyone else! There is an art to approaching power without looking like you're auditioning for groupie status. Here's the secret: You don't chase power. You align with it. When someone powerful is being swarmed, the worst thing you can do is elbow your way into the chaos. That's not presence—that's panic.

Instead, position yourself as "near but not needy." Stand just outside their current circle, close enough to be seen yet far enough to give them breathing room. Angle your body slightly toward them but stay engaged in your own conversation or calmly observe the room. This creates what's called "peripheral presence." They'll clock you, even if it's subconsciously. You're not vying for attention; you're commanding your own.

Take Dana, for example. At a major tech event, she wanted to connect with a CEO everyone was swarming. Instead of jumping into the crowd, she positioned herself five feet away, chatting confidently with someone else. At just the right moment, when the crowd thinned and the CEO's energy dipped, she turned slightly, caught his eye, and offered a simple, “You’ve been holding court all night; mind if I steal one minute?” He smiled and said, “Only if you promise to make it interesting.” She did. They talked. She got the follow-up meeting. That’s how you stand out: not by pushing, but by signaling calm competence, impeccable timing, and presence that doesn’t beg but invites.

This one is for folks who might be new on the job and don’t have their own office, or who work in a hybrid environment where you choose a desk when you arrive. How and where you set up speaks volumes before you even open your laptop.

Let me paint you a picture. Jasmine walks in, scans the room, and heads to a desk that faces the entrance, near a window with natural light. She sets her things down with calm intention, posture upright, and most importantly, her back is to a wall so she can see what’s going on and her face is visible to anyone walking through the space. From the moment she sits, her setup says: “I’m aware, I’m engaged, and I take myself seriously.” It’s not a bold move; it’s simply strategic. She’s placed herself where she can see what’s going on, where people can see her, and where she feels grounded.

Now let’s look at Darren. He arrives just after Jasmine and grabs the first desk he sees, leaving a trail of blueberry muffin crumbs behind him. His back is to the door and he’s facing a wall, half-shielded behind a monitor. He slouches into his chair, AirPods in, head down. Nothing about his physical positioning says, “I’m here to participate.” If anything, it reads more like: “Please pretend I’m not here so I can eat my muffin in peace while listening to the latest episode of my favorite podcast.”

Both workers might be equally smart and equally capable, but their workspace choices send completely different nonverbal messages. One is signaling presence and quiet authority. The other is fading into the background. And in rooms where opportunities are often given to the person who's simply noticed, that difference matters. And it's Jasmine whose face is forward and visible to everyone; so which of these two is going to get noticed by the Big Boss first when there's an opportunity to be doled out?

Finally, we're going to talk about one of the most important positions of power. There are times when a situation is so tough and so loaded that you need to activate your core power zone. The core power zone includes your abdomen, hips, and lower body, basically everything that keeps you physically grounded. Think of it as your body's anchor to the earth. When this zone is stable and engaged, it projects internal strength, certainty, and calm control. You become rooted, both literally and psychologically. This position matters because when you're negotiating, asserting your worth, or navigating a power dynamic, how you stand or sit is just as important as what you say. This is your silent signal that says, "I am immovable. I am not here to be shaken." Feeling rooted can also help keep your eyes on the prize—so you won't break down and yell, express anger, or feel overcome by frustration.

Take Ava, a creative director who had been doing the job of two people for six months. When she finally sat down with her boss to talk compensation, she didn't cross her legs or perch on the edge of her chair. She grounded both feet flat on the floor, spine straight, hands resting calmly on the table. No shifting, no fidgeting. Just her calm, rooted posture, which made her feel unshakable—and that energy translated. She wasn't just asking for more. She was making it clear she expected it.

Or Malik, a real estate broker negotiating with a tough client trying to undercut him on commission. Instead of reacting, Malik slowly stood, planted his feet hip width apart, and leaned slightly forward with his palms pressed lightly on the table. His stance was open, centered, and stable—his voice measured as he explained why that wouldn't work. That single movement changed the dynamic. The client backed down, and the full commission stayed on the table.

I know we're not talking about tennis, but if you want to see the core power zone mastered in motion, let yourself draw inspiration from Serena Williams. Her stance on the court is pure embodiment of grounded strength: feet planted, torso centered, movement controlled and deliberate. Even when the pressure is sky-high, she holds her ground like a magnitude nine earthquake couldn't send her off-kilter. That same presence can translate off the court—into any room, conversation, or confrontation.

That's the power of the core. When your lower body is stable, your upper body can deliver. You're not leaking nervous energy. You're radiating self-possession. I'll keep saying it: You never need to be the loudest in the room. You just need to be the most grounded. When you activate your core power zone, you hold space differently—calm, certain, and commanding, even when you are silent.

And listen, all this positioning isn't about manipulation; it's about fluency. It's about knowing how to work *with* the human brain, not against it. It's about understanding that presence isn't accidental; it's intentional. Where you stand, where you sit, where you flow...all of it communicates something before you've even opened your mouth. Positioning yourself strategically means you're no longer waiting for permission to participate; you're already part of the room's rhythm. So, the next time you walk into that boardroom, that office, that cocktail party or café where something important might happen, don't just default to safety. Pause. Read the room. Ask yourself: "Where is the energy gathering?"; "Who's commanding attention?" And "Where can I place myself so I'm not just watching things unfold, but ready to step into the action?" You don't need to shout to be noticed. You don't need to overcompensate to be respected. You just need to place yourself—deliberately, calmly, confidently—and let your presence do the rest. Because the person who understands the power of positioning doesn't just take up space. They shift it.

***Let me ask you this:***
***Are you set up for power on video calls?***

*Zoom and other video platforms have changed the way we work, in many ways for the better—but they are also rife with pitfalls. You will not come off as a confident queen and in control if you don't take some measures to ensure your presence on video is as powerful as it is in person.*

*First, you are not in witness protection. That gorgeous face needs to be well lit, ideally with light coming from the front or slightly from the side. Avoid backlighting, which can cast shadows. Appearing like a big blur, as if you're trying to keep your identity secret, will distract from your message. Natural light from a window or a ring light is your friend. We don't want to see your mess either. If you cannot keep your workspace tidy, embrace virtual backgrounds. I use several virtual backgrounds that feature chic, elegant, neutral-colored furnishings. Never having to worry if your kids' sporting equipment is in the background is a time and stress saver.*

*Nodding occasionally while listening is a simple nonverbal cue that shows you're present and attentive without interrupting. It shows you're engaged and following the conversation, not filling out your expense report. Look at the camera, not the screen, when speaking. This mimics eye contact with others in real life, which will convey confidence and attentiveness. The eyebrow flash—the raising of the eyebrows—will indicate nonverbally that you may be receptive to an idea. Do not keep looking at yourself. Be aware of excessive facial touching or playing with your hair; these self-touch gestures are like pacifiers—used to calm stress—and have no place in a meeting. If you find your own image distracting, turn yourself off!*

*Gestures are especially useful on Zoom. Use natural hand gestures to emphasize points while speaking to come off as dynamic and involved. But don't overdo it. Keep gestures at a moderate pace and mostly within the frame of the camera. As always, a confident tone of voice supports confident body language. Speak clearly, at a steady pace, and with a firm tone that doesn't sound rushed or hesitant. Some folks tend to speak louder and more abruptly on a video call. Make sure you aren't the Loud Talker.*

*Looking good on Zoom isn't just about vanity; it's about presence, credibility, and connection. In a world where first impressions are made in pixels, poor lighting, sloppy posture, or wandering eyes can subtly undermine your authority. The goal? Show up sharp, engaged, and intentional...because on camera, everything is magnified.*

## CHAPTER TEN

# The Subtle Art of Mirroring

Let's talk about one of the most underestimated, wildly effective, and borderline magical tools in the body language arsenal: mirroring. No, I'm not talking about mimicking someone like a mime or playing a game of copycat with your coworker until HR gets involved. I'm talking about the subtle art of aligning your energy and your body language with someone else's to create instant rapport, trust, and connection. Mirroring is what people who just "click" do without even thinking. It's what happens when two friends lean in at the same angle, sip their drinks in sync, or burst into laughter while unconsciously touching their hair at the same time. It's human harmony. And when done deliberately but softly—it's one of the fastest ways to get someone to feel safe with you, seen by you, and subtly drawn to you.

Let's start with Jess. Jess works in sales, and when I say she can sell ice to a polar bear, I mean it. Her secret weapon? It's not her pitch. It's not her PowerPoint. It's how she mirrors other people. Jess walks into a meeting, reads the room in two seconds flat, and adjusts her tone, pace, and body to reflect the energy of the person she's talking to. If her client is sitting back, arms loose, voice mellow, Jess softens her own body. If the client is animated, leaning forward, talking with their hands? Jess picks up her pace ever so slightly, mirroring the enthusiasm but never in a way that feels forced. She doesn't morph into a clone. She adapts, like tuning in to the same frequency. And it works. People feel comfortable around Jess, and comfort opens wallets.

The reason mirroring works is that people are drawn to what's familiar. We feel safer when we see ourselves reflected, even subtly, in someone else. Our brains register similarity as belonging, and belonging builds trust. That's why mirroring is so effective: It's nonverbal rapport in motion. But this isn't about being a human chameleon. The art is in the nuance. Case in point: Devin.

Devin works in politics—he wears a slick, perfectly tailored suit, has a killer handshake, and is terrifyingly charming. But when he first started out, he didn't understand the finesse of mirroring that is critical to pulling it off. He thought, "Okay, I'll just copy people, and they'll like me." Wrong. He once sat down with a donor who had a calm, almost regal stillness about her. Devin, trying to match it, went overboard. He slowed his speech to a crawl, barely moved, and ended up looking like he was about to faint. She asked if he was feeling all right. Not the effect he was going for. So we worked on it.

I told him, "Mirroring isn't mimicry. It's about attunement. It's a slow dance, not a flash mob. Start by aligning the rhythm...breathing, energy, the general posture. You're creating resonance, not replicating a pose." One night, he tried again. Different donor; different approach. This person was sharp, intense, and she leaned forward when she spoke. So Devin did too, but with subtlety. He matched her eye contact, adjusted his pacing, and let his gestures echo hers just slightly. She leaned in. He leaned in. Her voice rose. So did his. They clicked and the big donation was secured.

Another one of my favorite examples is Alina, a rising star at a tech start-up. She was trying to bond with the company's gruff, emotionally distant CTO who spoke in short, clipped sentences and never made eye contact. Instead of trying to dazzle him with bubbly small talk, Alina mirrored his tone, using slightly shorter sentences, more technical language, less filler. She didn't copy him, but she dialed down her usual warm tone just enough to land on his frequency. Over time, he began opening up. Now she's his go-to for big-picture brainstorming. She didn't bulldoze her way in. She matched the gatekeeper's rhythm until he opened the gate himself.

Now let's swing back into the dating world for a moment. Because if you've ever locked eyes with someone across a room, started talking, and noticed you are both suddenly leaning against the same table leg or sipping your drinks in sync, you've experienced the magic of unconscious mirroring. Take Serena.

Serena had been on a string of lackluster dates and came to me feeling like no one really connected with her. I asked her to try something different on her next date; not to change anything about herself, but to be more aware. Watch how he moves, I told her. Match his tone. Don't force anything. Just reflect his energy lightly.

Soon she went on a date with a guy named Peter. He was relaxed, leaned back in his chair, his laugh easy, shoulders open. So she let herself relax too. She mirrored his posture, slowed her pace, and matched the rhythm of their conversation. Nothing drastic. Just tuning in. By the end of the night, Peter said, "I had a great time. I'd really like to see you again." Exactly.

Mirroring works best when the person you're engaging with doesn't even realize it's happening. Because it's not about tricking anyone; it's about connecting. It's about saying, without words, "I see you. I'm with you." It's emotional glue.

And yes, this works in leadership too. Ever watched a great leader walk into a room of tense employees? They don't barge in with elevated Tony Robbins energy while everyone else is spiraling. They match the tension first, acknowledge it with their body, their tone, and then, slowly, they lead the energy upward. That's advanced mirroring. Meet the room where it is, then guide it to where you want it to go. One of the best examples of mirroring comes from former First Lady, bestselling author, and speaker Michelle Obama. Watch her in any setting, on a couch with Jimmy Fallon, in a classroom with kids, or onstage with a room full of CEOs. She knows exactly how to mirror the room's energy just enough to connect, but not so much that she ever loses her own authority. She leads with presence, not performance.

But beware. Auntie Linda needs to let you know there is a dark side to mirroring. And that's when it gets manipulative: when someone mirrors you to gain trust they *haven't earned*, to slip past your defenses and bend you toward their agenda. It's fake rapport and, eventually, people feel the glitch. The energy won't land because it's not rooted in sincerity. Think of the sleazy salesperson who matches your every move like a weird shadow. Creepy. That's not mirroring. That's mimicry with bad breath. So how do you keep your mirroring clean, honest, and effective? Start with intention. If your goal is to make someone feel seen, heard, and at ease, you'll naturally keep your mirroring light, respectful, and grounded. You'll adjust to them, but you won't disappear.

The real beauty of mirroring is that it's like a whisper in a crowded room; it doesn't demand attention, but it pulls people in. It's a form of presence, not pressure. A form of influence, not insistence. It's the art of saying, "We're in sync," without ever needing to say it out loud. And once you start practicing this? You'll see it everywhere. You'll catch couples mirroring each other's head tilts in line for coffee. You'll notice which coworkers sync up during meetings and which ones sit like they're on different planets. You'll start tuning in to your own habits when you fold your arms because someone else did, when you mirror someone's laugh or cross your legs the same way. It's all data. All connection.

So next time you're in a room with someone you want to connect with, whether it's a client, a crush, a colleague, or your cousin's weirdly intimidating new boyfriend, give it a try. Tune in.

Mirror their tone. Reflect their rhythm. Match their energy just enough to say, "I get you." Not loudly. Not desperately. Just clearly, quietly, masterfully. Welcome to the mirror game. Play it well, and the world will feel just a little more aligned with you.

***Let me ask you this: Do you work on sharpening your observation skills?***

*Most people are too caught up in their own internal chatter to truly notice what's unfolding around them, but to become a master of mirroring (and actually to read all forms of NVC), you need to be observant. This will help you mirror someone subtly, without going over the top and being mistaken for a mime. Developing keen observation skills requires you to train yourself to slow down, tune in, and absorb the details others so easily miss. Start by watching how people walk into a room, where they place their hands when they're nervous, how their expressions shift mid-conversation. It's about looking for patterns, not just isolated movements. Like any skill, it gets sharper with practice: Observe strangers on the subway, colleagues in meetings, couples on a date nearby. Don't judge; just notice. Treat the world like your training ground.*

*Nonverbal cues reveal more than words ever will. Honing your observation skills will help you decode a person's posture, facial expressions, or subtle shifts in energy, and you'll gain access to what's really going on beneath the surface. You can detect hesitation when someone's words say, "Yes," but their body says, "I'm not sure." You'll sense when someone's guarded, attracted, intimidated, or about to lie. It's not about being manipulative; it's about being aware. Possessing strong observation skills is like having emotional intelligence in 3D. It makes you a better communicator, a sharper leader, and a more intuitive friend or partner. In short, it gives you the upper hand in almost every human interaction. Here are a few easy ways to sharpen your observation skills and get better at reading nonverbal communication:*

- *People-watch with purpose. Go to a café, airport, or park and spend ten minutes observing others without distraction. Notice how they sit, gesture, and express emotion. Ask yourself: "What might they be feeling?"; "What's their energy saying?"*
- *Watch shows with the sound off. You know this is my personal favorite. Turn off the volume on a TV show or movie and try to follow the emotional story line using only facial expressions, gestures, and body language. Then replay it with sound to see how accurate your read was.*
- *Start a daily "tells" journal. After social interactions, jot down what nonverbal cues you noticed, such as shifts in posture, tone of voice, microexpressions, and how the person's behavior aligned (or didn't) with what they said.*
- *Mirror practice. Spend a few minutes in front of a mirror each day making different facial expressions on purpose. Learn what your own body looks like when you're feeling stressed, excited, guarded, or open. Knowing your own baseline helps you spot deviations in others.*

- *Ask curious follow-ups. In safe, trusted settings, try gently asking friends about their reactions: "You paused before answering just now. Were you thinking something else?"*

*The more you connect body language with truth, the faster your pattern recognition improves.*

## CHAPTER ELEVEN

# Breaking Through the Bias

Biases are mental shortcuts our brains use to make sense of the world quickly, but they can lead us to form unfair or inaccurate judgments about people, situations, or ideas. We all have them, no matter the color of our skin or where we come from. They're shaped by our experiences, upbringing, culture, media, and even the groups we belong to. While they mostly operate beneath our awareness, they often lead us to favor certain ideas, people, or groups over others. For example, you might assume someone is less competent because of how they dress or feel, and you might be more comfortable around someone who shares your background without realizing why. It doesn't mean we're bad people; it means we're human. Our brains are wired to categorize information to avoid overload, and in doing so, we can unconsciously favor some people or perspectives while discounting others. At its most basic level, you might unknowingly have a preference for people who went to the same college as you, but on the other end of the bias spectrum there's full-blown racism. Our biases start to complicate things because they don't just live in our thoughts; they show up in our bodies. Whether we realize it or not, the assumptions we carry can subtly leak out and become visible through our nonverbal communication.

Sometimes biases stir up negative reactions within ourselves that can cause us to shoot ourselves right in the foot. For example, Pilar nearly lost out on her biggest career move because of a bias that held too much power over her. In an interview with a partner at a highly competitive branding company in New York City, a simple question touched a very hot nerve that immediately made her angry. When the partner thanked her for coming in and casually asked, "Do you live in Manhattan or Brooklyn?" Pilar was surprised to feel herself getting revved up—in other words, the woman was *furious.* She could feel her face turning red and without knowing it she crossed her arms in front of her in a defensive posture. She could practically feel the laser beams coming out of her eyes. Pilar had recently moved from Brooklyn to New Jersey, and she had convinced herself that the most powerful New Yorkers believed the sun revolves around those two boroughs—and because she now lived elsewhere, she was lesser somehow. Comments such as "Jersey is too far away" or "Why would you ever leave a place as cool as Brooklyn?" made her blood boil. She worked hard and was successful, but upgrading her one-bedroom apartment to a brownstone was totally out of reach, so she moved her family across the river to where they could afford a beautiful home.

She didn't like to admit it, but she carried an internal bias toward folks who were born rich, got help from their parents, went to Ivy League schools (so they had better connections to access higher-paying jobs), and even toward people who worked in higher paying fields like finance! So when the partner asked that casual icebreaker of a question, her body was reacting as if he had said, "You live in New Jersey? That means you are less worthy than Ivy League graduates with trust funds such as myself."

Thankfully, Pilar recognized that her reaction to the question was inappropriate. She took a big breath—this was *her issue*, not his. She didn't even know where this man lived; they could be neighbors for all she knew! She brushed off her anger, pulled herself together, ultimately had a great interview, and got the job. Turns out she wasn't the only person at the company who lived in New Jersey either.

If you feel your bias getting in the way like Pilar's almost did, run through this short list of questions to regain control. Before you speak or act, hit the BRAKE—it helps slow down snap judgments and brings awareness to how bias might be influencing your negative response.

BRAKE

**B**—Body language: How is my body reacting right now? Am I leaning in or pulling away?
**R**—Reasoning: Am I responding based on facts or assumptions?
**A**—Affect: What emotion is driving this—fear, discomfort, irritation?
**K**—Knowledge: Do I really know this person or situation, or am I filling in gaps with a stereotype?
**E**—Equality: Am I giving this person the same openness and respect I'd offer someone I naturally relate to?

While Pilar's example shows how our own biases can hurt us by blocking opportunities, finding yourself on the other end of the biased thinking can be much worse.

Skylar and Jordan walked into an upscale fashion magazine for a pitch that could change everything for their budding careers, and they both felt the weight of the moment. Skylar, a young white woman with a sharp eye for digital storytelling, adjusted her blazer and strode confidently forward. Jordan, a young Black woman with an impressive portfolio and a vision for amplifying underrepresented voices, was right at her side. The receptionist barely glanced at Jordan but offered Skylar a warm smile. "Welcome. How can I help you?" she chirped, directing her words only to her. As they waited, fashionably dressed employees walked past, some nodding at Skylar while others barely acknowledged Jordan's presence. When they were finally ushered into the boardroom, the shift became even more obvious. The editor in chief leaned in when Skylar spoke, nodding along, hands relaxed, fingers steepled in interest. But when Jordan expanded on their concept, the editor in chief's expression tightened, she crossed her arms, and she pressed her lips together. One executive made it no secret that she was sending texts on her phone during Jordan's presentation. Jordan noticed it all, the microexpressions of dismissal and the subtle shifts of body language that said, "You don't belong here." Skylar felt it too, but in a different way. She was being welcomed, listened to, and encouraged. Jordan was being *tolerated* at best. By the end of the meeting, their pitch was accepted but not without an unspoken understanding between the two women. The door had opened, but not evenly. Jordan had to push her way through. Women like Jordan (as well as other BIPOC individuals) are subject to the ill effects of biases every day...and yes, often bias is actually blatant racism.

I know exactly what that feels like. I was a keynote speaker at a major conference in Maryland, and I was waiting behind the stage for my cue to go on when I heard the words "Can you get me a cup of coffee?" It took a few seconds to realize the request was aimed at me. The Caucasian man apparently needed a pick-me-up, so he decided to ask the well-dressed Black woman in designer heels to get him a coffee. Nothing about me signaled that I was a backstage handler. I was wearing a bright, emerald-colored St. John pantsuit, Ferragamo shoes, and my gold Rolex. He simply had no awareness.

I know many of my BIPOC people recognize this experience and it hurts. I know my disabled peeps, LGBTQ+ friends, and all my other friends who have been othered feel it too. I constantly get asked by y'all how you can maintain strong NVC in rooms where you are overlooked or not welcomed fully because of who you are. It's a very tough question to answer, and I'm going to do my best to help you take your power back. I've worked in jobs where I was the only Black woman salesperson on the team, so trust me: I know the bias well.

I told the man, "I don't work here, but I believe you can get coffee over there," and pointed in the direction of the craft services table. The host began to announce me and list my accolades, and I threw a little side-eye at the man. "That's me." I couldn't be bothered to turn back to see the expression on his face when he realized I was the speaker. I took a breath, got up onstage, and did my thing. No idea whether that man got his coffee or not; I was too busy advising an audience of high-net-worth individuals on how to maximize their NVC for greater success. I hope he learned something. But more important was how I left that experience. It felt as if he did not see me.

Biases show themselves in different ways. You can be hit with one comment, like that of Mr. Coffee, out of nowhere and feel tilted off your game for a minute, or you can be bombarded by these aggressions on a daily basis, having to deal with people at work or in ongoing circumstances that can feel crushing. Many of us wish we had ways to shield ourselves from these issues, but they are constant and unnerving. Women experience them in predominantly male industries. People of color experience them in majority white spaces. I can't stop biased people from entering your life, but I can give you the secret tips of what to look out for in their physical appearance so as to protect your well-being. With these tips you can decide when and how to remove yourself from these people and avoid low-energy interactions.

First, you might experience what I call "the turn away." The person is consistently turning their body away from you, crossing their arms, or walking away from you (as well as others who are of a different race or ethnicity). Then there are those who will avoid or minimize eye contact, which is so disrespectful. No, baby, you're not imagining it. Research in social psychology shows that racial biases can influence nonverbal behaviors, such as eye contact. For instance, a study by Wilhelm Hofmann and others found that participants with higher implicit racial bias scores showed less eye contact and more stiffness when interacting with individuals of different racial backgrounds.

You may also encounter microexpressions in the form of a brief frown, a grimace, or raised eyebrows that appear in split-second facial expressions that reveal negativity, judgment, or discomfort—even if the person expressing them isn't aware of his own bias! Sometimes you'll be hit with a cluster of signals..."the scold," a condescending, impatient, or dismissive tone, mixed with "the stand back"—someone visibly inching away from you or placing an object between the two of you. Think holding a briefcase in front of themselves or purposefully moving to the other side of a table. Once you've studied these cues, you'll see the signals and realize, "I am in a room with people who do not completely welcome me." And baby, that's putting it nicely.

Bias is like a rapidly mutating infection—it spreads quickly, grows stronger, and does great harm. These insidious subtle cues, gestures, and behaviors that communicate prejudice may be silent, but their impact is loud. Girl, I was busy after the pandemic consulting with countless BIPOC professional women who expressed hesitation about going back to the office, and it wasn't just about the convenience of working from home. I have listened to hundreds of women of color who work in predominantly white offices describe a feeling of being watched at work. They were convinced someone was paying attention and noticing their behavior: taking note when they got up to get coffee or use the bathroom or watching to see if they took long lunches or made calls on their personal phones. When BIPOC people sense they're being spied on at work, it can feel like they need to adapt to the dominant culture. A woman may start wondering if she's being judged for wearing her hair natural or in braids. She may worry that, due to her tone, she's being unfairly labeled as "aggressive."

This expectation to conform takes a toll and can impact performance.

I was giving a workshop on the basics of body language to a group of employees and their leaders at a company in the Deep South. The workshop was going well, there was positive energy, and everyone was having a good time. Also, I had a plan. I asked the executives to leave the room so the employees could have a breakout session. Once the managers were gone, I had the employees practice giving a short presentation, and I gave them feedback about their nonverbals. A Black man, Coach, held his head high and spoke strongly—the deep register of his voice adding a sense of richness and power. Overall, he exuded total confidence.

I asked the executives to come back in, and had Coach repeat his presentation with the Big Bosses in the room. Coach began his presentation, but the confident man was replaced with a terrified *American Idol* contestant, shuffling his feet back and forth, staring at the ground, barely able to speak. What happened? In that moment I said something no other body language expert could have said to a person of color. I was not messing around, and I whispered into his ear, "You are not on the plantation. Get your head out of the noose."

In that moment, his self-awareness of how his nonverbals shaped his message to the world hit him like a bolt of lightning. I swear it was like the moment in the movie *E.T.* when E.T. touches the dead flower and it pops back to life. I should never have had to say something so shocking to anyone, but this man's performance and potential were being trampled by his exposure to acculturative stress. As soon as his white bosses were out of the room and he was out of the so-called line of fire, his presentation was brilliant, buoyed by his strong NVC.

Another potential tactic I can offer is stillness, which is a reclaiming tool everyone should have in their arsenal. When you're being underestimated, misjudged, or dismissed, especially in biased spaces, your reaction becomes part of the story people tell about you. That's the trap. And that's why stillness is such a powerful act of resistance. In a moment where your identity or competence is being challenged, your instinct may be to overcompensate: to smile more, talk faster, soften your tone, explain your credentials, or even shrink your presence to avoid appearing "difficult" or "defensive."

But when you resist that urge and choose stillness instead, your body language begins to rewrite the narrative. For people who have historically felt the need to prove themselves—BIPOC individuals, women in male-dominated fields, LGBTQ+ individuals, anyone whose presence disrupts the status quo, anyone who's felt the pressure to "perform" their competence—stillness is an act of reclamation. You don't have to gesture more, speak faster, or smile harder to earn your space. You already belong. Stillness affirms that.

Tasha, a Black attorney in a corporate firm, shared how she used to overcompensate in meetings, talking fast, over-explaining, constantly nodding. She worried that if she wasn't visibly agreeable, her full power wouldn't be visible. But when she started practicing intentional stillness—sitting tall, pausing before speaking, and softening her nods—she noticed a shift. Colleagues began turning to her for clarity and guidance. Her stillness gave her words more weight. Think of stillness as a way of using your body to say, "I see what's happening here. And I am not here to prove my worth. I already know it."

Let me give you another example: During the 2021 Senate confirmation hearings for Judge Ketanji Brown Jackson, the first Black woman nominated to the US Supreme Court, she endured hours of intense, often patronizing questioning, much of it rooted in racial and political bias. Senators interrupted her, questioned her intelligence, and attempted to twist her words. But what stood out most was not just what she said, but also how she held herself. She didn't flinch. She didn't raise her voice. She didn't fidget or fill silences with nervous explanations. Instead, she sat upright, her hands folded or resting calmly, her facial expression neutral but alert. Even as the questioning became aggressive, she remained anchored. Her pauses before answering weren't hesitation; they were precision. She let silence do the heavy lifting. In those moments, her stillness became a mirror, reflecting the aggression back onto her challengers. She never gave them the emotional reaction they were hoping for, even when she was asked ridiculous questions, including what faith she follows (as a lawyer she obviously knew that question was unconstitutional) or when she was accused by Senator Marsha Blackburn of Tennessee of having a "hidden agenda." And in doing so, she displayed a kind of dignified control that transcended the setting. She wasn't just answering questions; she was commanding the room in her own way.

Let's be clear. Stillness is not about doing nothing. It's about doing *less*, but with intention. Feet grounded. Spine straight. Shoulders relaxed. Chin slightly lifted not in defiance, but in calm self-assurance. No fidgeting. No rushing to speak. No apology in your posture. It's the kind of control that communicates certainty and poise. It's the pause before you speak, the grounded way you enter a room, the obvious confidence in your posture when others are performing. It's the decision to let your body speak volumes with minimal movement. Think of stillness as the punctuation mark at the end of a bold sentence.

Stillness works because it contradicts our expectations. In high-pressure situations, people expect fidgeting, rushing, and nervous chatter. When someone chooses stillness instead, it breaks the pattern. The brain takes notice. Our nervous systems respond to calm. In fact, nonverbal cues like posture, movement, and silence strongly influence how others perceive our competence and confidence. A 2010 study from Harvard Business School found that expansive, grounded postures increased both perceived authority and actual risk tolerance. Stillness also creates a kind of psychological asymmetry. When one person stays still while another is agitated or trying to prove something, the still one appears more powerful. It's not about arrogance; it's about mastery. Stillness says, "I'm not here to chase approval. I *am* the approval."

Anytime you are facing conflict, stillness becomes your secret weapon. In heated moments, emotions rise, voices escalate, and people often speak without thinking. But if you can stay physically still, keep the shoulders relaxed, the face composed, and the breath steady, you instantly gain an edge. Your stillness signals control, which creates a calming ripple effect.

Isaac, a middle school principal in New Jersey, was known for his ability to de-escalate tense parent-teacher conferences. His trick? He never mirrored the energy of the angry parent and practiced stillness instead. He sat back slightly, kept his hands visible and still on the table, and listened without interrupting. He would then respond slowly, with a calm voice and extended eye contact. His physical stillness became an anchor in a storm of emotion. Eventually, parents started thanking him, not just for resolving the issues, but for making them *feel* heard. That's the power of calm.

For anyone navigating biased environments, this tactic can become a silent protest against systems that expect you to shrink or justify yourself. Stillness in the face of bias is not about playing nice. It's about reclaiming control of the narrative. It says: "You don't get to decide how I show up. *I decide*." Again, this doesn't mean silence is always the answer, but sometimes, before you speak, the pause—the power posture, the eye contact, the breath—*that* is what makes people lean in and makes your presence felt before your words ever arrive.

So, the next time you're being challenged in a space that wasn't built with you in mind, remember: You don't have to explain. You don't have to prove. You just have to hold. Hold your space. Hold your ground. Hold their gaze. And let the strength of your stillness speak volumes. In a world that's obsessed with doing the most, be the one who does less but means every move. Stillness signals that you trust yourself. That you don't need to prove your worth with volume or velocity. That you can hold a room without racing to catch up. The most powerful people in the world don't flail. They don't scramble. They hold. They pause. They *own* the space around them by mastering the space within them. Stillness is not the absence of energy—it's the most *concentrated* form of energy. Use it wisely.

I know that an interaction with a biased person can feel like you're talking to a preprogrammed robot who has exactly one setting: "I do not compute." I still remember the look of shock on the salesperson's face at Tiffany when I said, "Excuse me, I was here first." The store was empty except for me—and the white couple who entered a few minutes later. She ignored me but was ready to help this couple right away. When I pointed out the situation, it didn't seem to register at all (although Tiffany did send me a letter of apology). It was as if I and my money didn't matter at all. Often with the biased there is no interest in genuine understanding or even having a dialogue, reinforcing divisions rather than bridging them.

This skewed way of seeing the world often leads to missed opportunities for connection and growth, as the biased person is trapped by their own pathetic limitations. When faced with an unwelcoming situation and clueless person it's nearly impossible to keep your thoughts straight much less show your power, but baby, you must! *You do belong.* The room may clearly be unwelcoming, but *you have value.* Take up space. Sit tall and with confidence, knowing the utterly unique shade of your skin is a beautiful gift. No matter how ugly that room feels, hold your head high and maintain steady eye contact. No, you will not back down. Your body language should reflect your power, not diminish it. Speak with clarity and conviction, refusing to rush or apologize for taking the floor that is rightly yours.

If stillness will bring you the strength you need, use it to your advantage. A well-placed pause will force others to listen and process your wise words. Stillness is not silence. Stillness is strength! Command the space with intentionality, dressing in a way that makes you feel powerful in your body, positioning yourself as a key player, not an afterthought. If you sense pushback, don't shrink—ground yourself. Plant your feet apart, hold yourself in that commanding position, and know nothing can shake you. Their discomfort with your confidence is their problem, not yours. You don't need permission to be in the room. You *are* the value, and you can never let yourself forget that.

***Let me ask you this: What gets you all juiced up?***

*Dealing with the stress of racism is emotionally exhausting, and you must take care of your mental and emotional well-being. First, building a strong support system of trusted friends, family, parishioners, or colleagues who understand and validate your experiences can provide a safe space for processing feelings. Seeking therapy, particularly with culturally competent professionals, is another powerful way to manage racial trauma and stress. Talk to your pastor if that helps. It's also important to set boundaries in environments where racism or microaggressions occur; protect your mental health by knowing when to disengage. Finally, getting involved in advocacy or racial justice efforts can transform feelings of frustration into empowerment, allowing women to not only cope but also contribute to meaningful change. By focusing on self-compassion, support, and active engagement, women can better navigate the stress that comes with racism.*

*When I have an experience like I did with "Mr. Coffee," I know I have to do something special to keep myself strong and whole. I'll make time to get what I call "juiced up." Getting juiced up is my own version of self-care. It means tapping into what truly lights you up and fuels your passion, finding energy and inspiration in the things you love. Whether it's a creative project, a hobby, mindfulness, exercise, or travel…or a cause you're deeply committed to, getting juiced up can help you to recharge and reduce the emotional burden.*

*Now, I love a good spa day, a night at the theater, dancing, or, when life permits, a visit to the Ritz-Carlton on Lake Oconee in Georgia where I swear the beds have the magical power to lull a woman into a long, deep sleep. Harnessing your inner fire to keep going can help you stay healthy and balanced. When you immerse yourself in activities that resonate with your core, they become a source of strength, recharging you emotionally and mentally. This connection to what you love can uplift your spirit, remind you of your potential, and provide the fuel you need to overcome ANYTHING with enthusiasm and confidence.*

## CHAPTER TWELVE

# The Hush

The irony wasn't lost on me. Here I was, an internationally known public speaker, body language expert, and the woman who helps people find their voice without saying a word, suddenly unable to speak at all. A throat nodule shut me down. I couldn't coach; I couldn't perform, I couldn't do interviews. I couldn't even whisper encouragement to my clients, let alone command a stage. Just silence. Complete, humbling, echoing silence. At first, I panicked. My voice wasn't just a tool. It was my identity. My livelihood. My gift. How could I possibly lead others if I couldn't even speak?

But something extraordinary happened in that hush. With my words stripped away, my senses sharpened. My awareness deepened. I didn't stop communicating; instead, I evolved. I began to see even more than I had before. The tiniest shoulder drop. The millisecond pause before a forced smile. A blink too long, a breath too shallow, a hand twitching in midair. I could feel someone's anxiety before they knew they were feeling it. I could track a whole emotional journey in a five-second silence. Without my voice, I became more attuned to the conversation beneath the conversation, the one that was always happening, quietly and powerfully, through the body.

Silence, to my surprise, didn't create distance...it invited connection. People leaned in more. They slowed down to truly connect. They softened right in front of me. Without my voice to guide the exchange, they began to fill the space with their own vulnerability and intention. I watched them gesture more thoughtfully, search my eyes for understanding, and adjust their pace to meet me where I was. In those moments, I felt a different kind of closeness, one rooted not in words, but in effort. Strangers, clients, even friends who had once relied on me to lead the conversation began revealing parts of themselves I might never have seen otherwise. My silence became a mirror, reflecting back their desire to be understood. And what bloomed from that quiet was something I didn't expect: tenderness, trust, and a shared recognition that sometimes the deepest human connection happens when we stop trying to fill the silence—and simply listen inside it.

But this chapter of my life didn't just teach me something about stillness; it taught me something about strength. And this book, *Hush*, was never just about decoding body language or catching a lie or finally getting a second date (though you'll do all that and more). It's about claiming the full power that's been living inside you all along. Let's be real. You wouldn't have picked up this book if you weren't ready to step into something bigger. Maybe you were tired of being overlooked. Maybe you've been stuck in a cycle where your brilliance keeps getting buried under insecurity, self-doubt, or miscommunication. Maybe you know, deep down, that you are so much more than what people have been seeing.

*Hush* is your guide to finally showing the world who you are with crystal clarity. Because presence is power. Not noise. Not flash. Not trying too hard. Not shrinking to keep the peace. Real presence lives in the way you walk into a room, the way you hold eye contact, the way you breathe, the way you sit when it's time to speak, and the way you *don't* flinch when you're challenged. Every chapter in this book has been designed to help you strip away the habits that don't serve you and replace them with strategies that elevate you. This is about learning to tell the truth with your body—your *real* truth, not the story fear has been writing for you behind your back.

When I lost my voice, I found something deeper. A new layer of awareness. A sharpened edge. A spiritual kind of clarity. And that's the level of goodness I want for you in your life. I want you to understand what your body has been saying all along. I want you to take control of the silent messages you're sending out into the world, because those messages shape your relationships, your reputation, and your reality. This is not about being perfect. Auntie Linda does not believe in perfect! This is about being intentional. It's about making a powerful choice to walk through the world aligned. Aligned in what you say, what you believe, and what your presence declares before you speak. Because when your body and your purpose are in sync, baby, you become magnetic.

So if you've ever been told you were "too much" or "not enough"; if you've ever watched someone less talented get the role, the raise, the relationship, the recognition—this book was written for *you*. If you've ever wanted to be seen…not just noticed, but seen in your full light, *Hush* is your road map. Not to be louder, but to be clearer. Not to fake confidence, but to embody it. Not to perform power, but to radiate it.

You now hold the tools to shift how the world responds to you. Use them. Trust them. Practice them. Let them reshape how you show up, how you lead, how you love. Walk into that boardroom, that coffee date, that family dinner, that audition, that hard conversation…*any room* knowing you can hold the floor without ever raising your voice.

Because true power doesn't need to shout.

It stands tall.

It breathes deep.

It radiates.

And now, so do you.

Baby, you are the message. You are the signal. You are the spark.

Let the world hush and watch you rise.

# ACKNOWLEDGMENTS

Thank you to all of my past teachers, coaches and mentors, and instructors on human development and potential. Your expertise has enriched my life both personally and professionally.

Thank you to J. J. Newberry for your invaluable teachings and training. The late world-renowned spiritualist Lillian Cosby, thank you for seeing my God-given gifts and teaching me to develop and nurture those gifts at a higher level.

Thank you to the Body Language Institute for inviting me to be a guest expert instructor.

To my brother, sisters, nieces, and nephews as well as the rest of my family...thank you for your love and support as I made my way along in this journey.

A hearty thank-you to all the corporations, associations, organizations, HR/DEI champions, entrepreneurs, solopreneurs, and individual supporters I've had the pleasure of working with. I appreciate you all.

To the event planners, promoters, conference coordinators, and journalists, as well as the radio, TV, and podcast hosts who have supported my work for over three decades, thank you for being with me along the way.

A special thanks to the organizations who have honored me by inviting me multiple times to speak over the years: ColorComm, Corporate Counsel Women of Color, Odyssey, Power Networking Conference, PowHERful Foundation, eWomenNetwork, Thurgood Marshall College Fund, Black Enterprise Women of Power, National Urban League, National Sales Network, and Mindvalley University.

A special thanks to my faith-based family and community, Light of the World Christian Church and New Life Worship Center in Indianapolis, Indiana; Friendship West in Dallas, Texas; and Triumph Church, in Detroit, Michigan. I would also like to extend my gratitude to R. Thomas Schmidt and Ruemu Birhiray.

Special thanks to these agents of transformation for their unwavering commitment and support during the pandemic: Sandra Sims-Williams, Hosetta Coleman, Tiffany Smith-Anoa'i, Caroline Clarke, Cheryl Walker-Robertson, and Soon Mee Kim.

A special thanks to this extra-special group who encouraged and helped me get this book off the ground: JJ Virgin, Celeste Fine, and Kevin Anderson and Associates.

To Jaidree Braddix, head of publishing at ARC Collective and my super-agent. You are the best agent with a Zen-like gift for making everything work out. Your commitment and support through this process will never be forgotten. You are a jewel.

To my editor, Krishan Trotman, thank you for your determination, dedication, and relentless commitment to make sure this book was right. Your guidance and expertise were invaluable throughout this entire process. I'm glad we chose each other.

To the entire publishing team at Legacy Lit, thank you for your hard work and commitment: Tara Kennedy, Maya Lewis, Mahito Indi Henderson, Yasmin Mathew, Carolyn Kurek, Jane Herman, Erin Cain, Dana Li, Sheryl Kober, and Sara Schaller.

To Paula B. Vitale, thank you for being "revved up" on my behalf. The way you channel your fire and magic to shape, mold, and translate my dreams into words is truly remarkable. Your ability to ignite vision into language isn't just a talent…it's a true gift.

# NOTES

p28 Sylvia Ann Hewlett, in her book . . . : Sylvia Ann Hewlett, *Executive Presence: The Missing Link Between Merit and Success* (New York: HarperBusiness, 2014), 26.

p29 *Forbes* reports that people who use . . . : Carol Kinsey Goman, "5 Ways to Instantly Increase Your Leadership Presence," *Forbes*, January 18, 2016. https://www.forbes.com/sites/carolkinseygoman/2016/01/18/5-ways-to-instantly-increase-your-leadership presence/.

p29 A study from *Frontiers in Psychology* . . . : Judee K. Burgoon, Xinran Wang, Xunyu Chen, Steven J. Pentland, and Norah E. Dunbar, "Nonverbal Behaviors 'Speak' Relational Messages of Dominance, Trust, and Composure," *Frontiers in Psychology* 12 (2021). https://doi.org/10.3389/fpsyg.2021.624177).

p29 A study called "Nonverbal Communication in Close Relationships" . . . : P. Noller, "Nonverbal Communication in Close Relationships," in V. Manusov and M. L. Patterson, eds., *The Sage Handbook of Nonverbal Communication* (Sage Publications, 2006), 403–20. https://doi.org/10.4135/9781412976152.n21.

p33 A 2024 report by the National Alliance on Mental Illness . . . : National Alliance on Mental Illness (NAMI), "The 2024 NAMI Workplace Mental Health Poll," conducted by Ipsos, 2024. https://www.nami.org/support-education/publications-report/survey-reports/the-2024-nami-workplace-mental-health-poll/.

p42 According to a September 2024 article . . . : NeuroLaunch Editorial Team, "Blank Stare Psychology: Unraveling the Mystery Behind Expressionless Gazes," *NeuroLaunch*, September 14, 2024. https://neurolaunch.com/blank-stare-psychology/.

p45 A 2014 study from the University of Chicago . . . : Nicholas Epley and Juliana Schroeder, "Mistakenly Seeking Solitude," *Journal of Experimental Psychology: General* 143, no. 5 (2014): 1980–99. https://www.chicagobooth.edu/review/talk-to-a-stranger-itll-make-you-happier.

p45 A 2010 study published in *Social Psychological and Personality Science* . . . : Oscar Ybarra, Piotr Winkielman, Irene Yeh, Eugene Burnstein, and Kent Marzillier, "Friends (and

Sometimes Enemies) with Cognitive Benefits: What Types of Social Interactions Boost Executive Functioning?" *Social Psychological and Personality Science* 1, no. 3 (2010): 253–61. https://doi.org/10.1177/1948550610386808.

p62 A study published in 2024...: Zsófia Csajbók, Zuzana Štěrbová, Peter K. Jonason, and Lucie Jelínková, "Observed Aspects of Mate Value and Sociosexuality Account for Sex Differences in Acceptance of Undesirable Characteristics in Romantic Partners," *Archives of Sexual Behavior* (2024). https://doi.org/10.1007/s10508-024-02707-5.

p70 ...further studied by behavioral researchers Jason Rogers and Abbe Macbeth...: Jason Rogers and Abbe Macbeth, "Throwing Shade: The Science of Resting Bitch Face," *Noldus Information Technology,* October 2015. https://www.scribd.com/document/305542618/Rogers-J-Macbeth-A-2015-Throwing-Shade-The-Science-of-Resting-Bitch-Face.

p70 Responding to a question...: "73 Questions with Victoria Beckham," *Vogue*, January 8, 2015. https://www.vogue.com/video/watch/73-questions-ever-wonder-why-victoria-beckham-never-smiles.

p79 For instance, research published in the journal...: Daniel H. Lee, Joseph M. Anderson, and Jeffrey S. Shimamura, "Inferring Emotion from the Eyes: The Role of Eye Gaze Direction and Head Orientation," *Psychological Science* 23, no. 7

(2012): 692–97. https://www.psychologicalscience.org/news/releases/we-read-emotions-based-on-how-the-eye-sees.html.

p90 In a now legendary social psychology experiment . . . : Robert Levine, *The Power of Persuasion: How We're Bought and Sold* (Hoboken, NJ: Wiley, 2003), 36.

p90 More recently, security consultant and social engineer Chris Hadnagy . . . : Christopher Hadnagy, *Social Engineering: The Science of Human Hacking*, 2nd ed. (Hoboken, NJ: Wiley, 2018).

p93 In fact, a 2015 study . . . : Shwetha Nair, Mark Sagar, James J. Sollers III, Nathan S. Consedine, and Elizabeth Broadbent, "Do Slumped and Upright Postures Affect Stress Responses? A Randomized Trial," *Health Psychology* 34, no. 6 (2015): 632–41. https://doi.org/10.1037/hea0000146.

p110 Paul Ekman, the renowned American psychologist . . . : Paul Ekman, *Telling Lies: Clues to Deceit in the Marketplace, Politics, and Marriage*, 3rd ed. (New York: W. W. Norton, 2009), 45.

p126 In a 2010 study . . . : Kim B. Serota, Timothy R. Levine, and Franklin J. Boster, "The Prevalence of Lying in America: Three Studies of Self-Reported Lies," *Human Communication Research* 36, no. 1 (2010): 2–25. https://doi.org/10.1111/j.1468-2958.2009.01366.x.

p205 For instance, a study by Wilhelm Hofmann...: Wilhelm Hofmann, Tobias Gschwendner, Luigi Castelli, and Michael Schmitt, "Implicit Bias and the Nonverbal Display of Intergroup Attitudes: The Role of Interpersonal Distance," *Group Processes & Intergroup Relations* 11, no. 1 (2008): 69–74. https://doi.org/10.1177/1368430207084844.

p210 A 2010 study from Harvard Business School...: Dana R. Carney, Amy J. C. Cuddy, and Andy J. Yap, "Power Posing: Brief Nonverbal Displays Affect Neuroendocrine Levels and Risk Tolerance," *Psychological Science* 21, no. 10 (2010): 1363–68. https://doi.org/10.1177/0956797610383437.

# RAISING READERS

## Books Build Bright Futures

Thank you for reading this book and for being a reader of books in general. We are so grateful to share being part of a community of readers with you, and we hope you will join us in passing our love of books on to the next generation of readers.

**Did you know that reading for enjoyment is the single biggest predictor of a child's future happiness and success?**

More than family circumstances, parents' educational background, or income, reading impacts a child's future academic performance, emotional well-being, communication skills, economic security, ambition, and happiness.

Studies show that kids reading for enjoyment in the US is in rapid decline:

- In 2012, 53% of 9-year-olds read almost every day. Just 10 years later, in 2022, the number had fallen to 39%.
- In 2012, 27% of 13-year-olds read for fun daily. By 2023, that number was just 14%.

Together, we can commit to **Raising Readers** and change this trend. How?

- Read to children in your life daily.
- Model reading as a fun activity.
- Reduce screen time.
- Start a family, school, or community book club.
- Visit bookstores and libraries regularly.
- Listen to audiobooks.
- Read the book before you see the movie.
- Encourage your child to read aloud to a pet or stuffed animal.
- Give books as gifts.
- Donate books to families and communities in need.

BOB1217

**Books build bright futures**, and **Raising Readers** is our shared responsibility.

For more information, visit **JoinRaisingReaders.com**

Sources: National Endowment for the Arts, National Assessment of Educational Progress, WorldBookDay.com, Nielsen BookData's 2023 "Understanding the Children's Book Consumer"